Cooking for Me
and
Sometimes You

~

Also by Barbara-Jo McIntosh

Tin Fish Gourmet
Great Chefs Cook at Barbara-Jo's

Barbara-jo McIntosh lives in Vancouver, Canada, and is the proprietress of Barbara-Jo's Books to Cooks.

Cooking For Me
and
Sometimes You

A Parisienne Romance with Recipes

Barbara-jo McIntosh

Illustrations
Bernie Lyon

french apple press

I call this book *my little one*.
I dedicate it to you.
But mostly,
It's for me.

MY PATH TO PARIS

When I am despondent, I dream of Paris. When I am content, I dream of being in Paris, in love. I am adamant in my belief that we must concoct many dreams for ourselves. Some dreams we will develop and realize quickly, while others might simmer on the back burner for years. And occasionally we will form an attachment with a dream for a while, but eventually we may lose heart and end up dumping it in the bin.

My dream of living, cooking and eating in Paris for a month has been on the back burner for far too long. But now, it is time to turn the knob on the hob to high and make this dream sizzle.

And so I find myself living my dream. I have come to Paris with many plans and much enthusiasm but, unfortunately, very little ability to communicate in the language of the people who live here. This is sad for me, as I love to talk and I embarrass easily when I cannot be understood. But while I am here I hope to be able to hone my skills in both patience and observation, which just might enhance my French vocabulary.

With this story of my month in Paris, I intersperse recipes that have been inspired by the food I have bought in the markets, meals I have eaten in restaurants, cookbooks I admire and conversations I have had with others about food. I share them here – gladly – with you.

I have come to Paris alone. I am a single woman of a certain age. I have chosen a single life, and though I have loved deeply, thinking at times it would be wonderful to investigate the mysteries of marriage, I have remained successfully single. When I say "successfully," I mean that generally I am happy with my own company and have not allowed the stigma that society can attach to unmarried women like me to interfere with my quest for joy.

I have also come to Paris to cook. When I was young and lived at home with my mother, I was not allowed to cook. My mother was an independent career woman with feminist ideals, but I don't think that was why she discouraged me from cooking; rather, I think Mother was more concerned about economics. She always felt that I was one of the few people in the world who should have been born with a silver spoon in their mouth because my desires in all matters, particularly when I was preparing food, were too extravagant. So, naturally, when I left the family home I was determined to prove her — and the rest of the family — wrong, and show that I was able to take care of myself, especially in the kitchen.

I laugh now, remembering the first dinner I cooked for my boyfriend of the era. The roast beef was ready at 6:00 p.m., but the potatoes were cooked at 5:00 p.m. and the carrots and broccoli were perfect at 4:00 p.m. How this happened I would never figure out. But I was not discouraged, and I began to take cooking classes and to clip recipes from magazines and newspapers. When my mother observed my efforts to become proficient in the kitchen, she presented me with a beautiful French cookbook that included classical French preparations, table settings of the French aristocracy and all the proper details deemed necessary for entertaining in the home.

The years bubbled along. I fell in love with a man who was involved with fish, which led to many meals from the sea, and eventually inspired me to write *Tin Fish Gourmet*, a cookbook I developed over the years based on fresh fish recipes that I adapted to celebrate fish from the can. I have fond memories of those years, but the pain of my heart breaking when the love affair with my fish-man ended still lingers. Though our relationship changed, we remained a part of each other's lives for thirty years, and when he died, shortly after my mother died, I was devastated.

It is often said that food heals the soul that has been shattered. Was that why I aborted my original career choices of journalism and social work to embrace café society? I spent years working for Vancouver restaurateur Umberto Menghi, loving the way Italians embraced their food and the importance of eating together when the work was done – no matter what had happened earlier in the day or how angry you had been with one another, because in the end, you shared your meal, healed your wounds and carried on, well nourished.

While I am not one to regret choices made along the way, I sometimes wonder how my life would have evolved if I had remained for a longer stretch in that Latin environment. But I didn't; I was impatient to evolve, and so I moved along, working in the hotel business for a few years, attending culinary school to learn the basics of French classical cuisine, eventually tossing my shingle into the sky, letting it bounce about in ventures involving catering, designing unique events and starting my own restaurant.

That restaurant – Barbara-Jo's Elegant Home Cooking – was a gem. It was an extension of my dining room, with seating for thirty-four guests. But when the lease was up for renewal, just over three years after I opened the doors, I knew it was time to let my head take over my heart and say goodbye to this dream.

Closing the restaurant was difficult – one of those occasions when a healthy, supportive relationship would have been extremely welcome. But soon after my mourning subsided, I told myself it was time to put everything I had learned into a magic lamp and rub it really hard until my next dream popped out. Well, that's not exactly how it happened, but somewhat magically I dreamed a new dream to open my cookbook shop, complete with a kitchen. I knew people would think me bonkers for coming up with this plan, so for just over a year, while I investigated the possibilities of creating this business, I confided in just a few people. And here I am – twelve years later – fully ensconced in the world of cookbooks, and meeting and becoming friends with chefs and authors around the world. We host cooking events with these chefs and authors who contribute incredibly to fulfilling my dream of educating our community about the pleasures of eating well and cooking for family, friends and most importantly, yourself.

But now it is time for Paris – to realize another long-held dream.

Paris, a city overflowing with wonderful ingredients to cook with. If you are truly in love with food, you can be assured you will be in love with Paris. And if you are truly in love with love, a love for beauty that runs deep through all genres, Paris will happily take you by the hand and accommodate you if you are willing to risk your heart.

So, I offer to you this *Parisienne Romance with Recipes*. It is my hope that as you read these pages, whether you are alone or not, you will learn to appreciate how loving food can be the catalyst for a happy relationship with life. It has been for me.

Bon appétit!

COOKING IN PARIS

When you rent a flat for month, be it in Paris or anywhere else, for simplicity's sake you will find yourself using similar ingredients in all of your recipes. If you don't follow this basic rule, you will find yourself spending a lot of money trying to emulate your kitchen at home. And you just don't need to do that.

I took my own advice while in Paris, and so you'll see that for the recipes I've included in this book I have tried to mix creativity with a practical pantry. All of them are simple and very pleasing for a solo cook to prepare. But I also wanted to feel proud enough of these dishes to serve them to anyone who just might happen to drop by to share my table.

This is not a seasonal cookbook, even though I created all of these recipes in February. But the ingredients I use here are all available, almost everywhere, almost all year round. Some may be extra agreeable in season: just think what the recipes using tomatoes will taste like in the summer!

Many of these recipes call for citrus salts, which I like to keep on hand for cooking at any time. My formula for these salts is simple. Be it lemon salt or orange salt, just add 1 part zest to 2 parts Maldon salt (Maldon is my favourite brand, but you can use any salt). Mix together, and cover what you do not use with plastic wrap.

To make espelette salt, mix together 1 teaspoon espelette pepper (a variety of chili pepper), 2 tablespoons Maldon salt and ½ teaspoon fresh French thyme leaves, chopped fine. Mix together. This mixture keeps well, though I never make large batches, unless I am giving them away for a gift with a copy of my book!

"If you ask me why I came to this Earth,
I'll tell you: I came to live out loud." – Émile Zola

3, FEBRUARY

As I arrive in Paris today, I think back to my first trip here in 1983; I entered the city in a Renault "le car" that I had rented for the summer to travel through Italy and France. Within minutes of getting behind the wheel, I hit another car as I tried to fit into the flow of a roundabout, and I decided then and there to get rid of the car and never try to drive in Paris again. The shin splints I moan about today, I proudly boast, were acquired on that inaugural trip, getting to know Paris on foot.

Today, I enter Paris by train, a mode of travel that accentuates my romantic desires to embrace the Paris I remember from books and films that were popular before travel by air became commonplace. My thoughts float to the Paris where lovers would meet each other at the train station, drink champagne in coupe glasses and march through the streets holding their unprotected baguettes with carefree abandon.

I left Vancouver hungry for Paris; I arrive ravenous, and the combination of a brilliant sky and chilly air create an intense desire to consume and nourish all that my heart and soul can hold. On my first trip to Paris, and on many subsequent visits, I was frustrated because I longed for a kitchen. I was fortunate enough to understand, even at a tender age, that when in a city where the culture is so dedicated to food, a happy way to nourish yourself is to bring the beautiful ingredients from the farmers' markets home, and cook. Today, I happily anticipate the kitchen awaiting me.

When I enter my rented flat, I immediately feel at home. I would love to have a grander room with high ceilings and a large balcony, but this building was originally constructed as a stable for the apartment block next door, and I am reminded of that every time I enter through the main door from the street, walking down a cobbled path that once felt the hooves and wheels of another era.

But this flat is most definitely French. Herringbone wood floors, beamed ceilings, antique furniture, guilt-framed mirrors and lots of windows. There is a desk at one of the windows overlooking the courtyard – the perfect place to write. I walk through the sitting room to the bedroom and know I am going to be very comfortable here.

Although I am tired, I am very anxious to explore the neighbourhood, and of course I do want to eat. Once I have walked a block, I realize, indeed, I am too tired to explore and decide to stop in a café and order a meal. The view from the window is stunning: Notre Dame to the right, Pont Saint Louis in front, and of course, the River Seine. Who was it who described the Seine as "never grey or green, always boiling"? But the presented menu at this café, in contrast, is pedestrian to say the least; I order a glass of Côtes du Rhône, a bowl of French onion soup and a salad. The meal is not good; as I will most likely repeat often, you can get a lot of bad food in Paris. I imagine the broth is from a can, and the onions have been produced en masse in some factory. The cheese, piled on the bread, and unctuously unappealing, cannot be good as there is just so much of it. The salad is composed of vegetables most likely taken from a package that was sitting in a warehouse for a few weeks, with an egg that, I can wager, has not been boiled in-house.

While I enthusiastically drink my wine, I play with my salad and hesitantly take a few spoonfuls of soup, then dream about the version I want to make (and eat) using red onions, rosé wine, Gruyère and homemade broth. I will accompany my soup with a mimosa salad using leeks instead of lettuce, an idea I want to adapt from Skye Gyngell's book, *A Year in My Kitchen*.

But really, I have long been aware of the cafés of Paris that take full advantage of the naive traveller, and under these fatiguing circumstances, I am not too troubled. So, I return to my flat, grateful for my own French kitchen, to unpack, bathe, sleep and dream about the month ahead.

Pink Onion Soup

This soup turns pink in the cooking, which is somehow fitting when I think of the feelings I was experiencing in my new (albeit temporary) home – young, naive and somewhat rebellious. I like to make a Gruyère tuile (a type of savoury cookie) to place on top of the soup.

Serves me and you

Peel two medium-size red onions, then cut them in half and slice into half moons, fairly thin. Place the slices in a bowl and toss with 2 tablespoons of rice flour and 1 teaspoon espelette salt.

In a medium-size saucepan set over medium-low heat, sauté the onion mixture for about 2 minutes. Add ½ cup rosé wine and reduce for about 45 seconds. Add 1½ cups vegetable stock. Bring to a boil, then reduce heat and simmer for about 20 minutes. Season to taste with pepper and, if desired, more salt.

Gruyère tuile topping

Grate 2 tablespoons of Gruyère cheese for each tuile, forming into rounds on a baking tray lined with parchment paper. Bake in oven set at 350° F/180° C for 10 minutes. Place on top of hot soup and serve.

Toast topping

If you prefer a more traditional finish for this soup, toast a piece of your favourite bread, cut off the crusts and trim the toast to make it as round as possible. Pour the soup into an ovenproof bowl. Place the toast on top of the soup and sprinkle with grated Gruyère. Place under the broiler for a few minutes until brown and bubbly.

Leeks Mimosa

Choose a fresh leek with green leaves and a creamy white top. If you are not lucky enough to procure one so delicate, be sure to cut off any tough green leaves and root ends. Cut the leek into ½-inch rounds. Place rounds in a bowl of cold water to wash off any lingering dirt.

Serves me

In a small saucepan, bring to boil enough water to cover the leek pieces. To the boiling water, add ¼ cup apple cider vinegar. Place the leeks into the boiling water. Reduce heat to a simmer and cook for 8 minutes. Remove the leeks from the water and plunge them into an ice bath for just 1 minute. Drain, and set aside.

Place a small egg in cold water in a saucepan and bring to a boil. Remove saucepan from heat and let the egg evolve into a hard jewel (about 10 minutes). Place the egg in cold water for 1 minute, then remove it from the water and peel. Grate the cooked egg with a micro plane grater or press it through a sieve. Set aside.

To make the vinaigrette, whisk together 1 tablespoon apple cider vinegar, ½ teaspoon Dijon mustard, 2 tablespoons extra virgin olive oil and 2 tablespoons grape seed oil. Add salt and pepper to taste.

To serve, place the leeks on a plate, cover with as much or as little vinaigrette as you desire, then sprinkle with grated egg.

4, February

Sleep does not come easily as I try to acclimatize to my new home thousands of miles and multiple time zones away from Vancouver. The telephone rings first at midnight, and though happy to hear a French voice welcoming me to Paris, I am not sure the time he chooses to call is appropriate.

A few hours later, the phone ringing awakens me again. I have left my cookbook shop in the care of my staff. Mostly, I am comfortable with this arrangement, but it is the first time in twelve years that I have taken a month away from my long-standing relationship – my business. At 4:30 a.m. I am reminded of that when I pick up the phone to take the call from back home. Is there a problem? Not at all.

One of the more satisfying initiatives that we began a few years ago at the shop is a reading club where we read books about food, memoirs and occasionally a novel in which food is strongly integrated into the narrative. We call the book club Eating Between the Leaves, and on this night the group is meeting and decide it would be humorous to call me to find out if I am indeed in Paris, alone. And, they want to tell me exactly what they think about the book they are discussing: *We've Always Had Paris… and Provence*, by Patricia and Walter Wells. The "libatious" laughter in the background does not amuse me, and I must admit I am not too genteel when I request that they not call me again in the wee hours of the morning.

But soon, the sun rises, and *oui*, I am in Paris. And though my bed is comfy and I could easily luxuriate in it for hours, I hurry to ready myself for a few hours of exploring.

I scout the neighbourhood for a café that I hope to frequent, and I soon discover a stylish spot on the Île Saint Louis, Le Lutétia. It appears jolly, with a Parisian clientele. The café long is superb so I order another, but I only devour one *pain au chocolat*. There is a pharmacy near the café – I need essentials. I ask the pharmacist about face cream; he asks if I am interested in anti-aging cream and I reply, most certainly. Then he asks my age, and in the carefree mood of the moment, I take eight years away.

As I stroll down the street of this idyllic island in the middle of Paris, in a dreamy state, I stop to breathe deeply and pinch myself. I find a pleasant grocer and purchase butter and yogurt, fruit and a few vegetables. I have heard that the butcher on this street is one of the best in Paris and I enter the shop to find a gaggle of hearty, rosy-cheeked men, proudly choosing just the right cut for their discerning customers. The *boulangerie*, the *pâtisserie*, the wine shop, the flower shop – all magnificent. Will I ever venture away from this street? Of course I will; this tony neighbourhood is very expensive, and as much as I love to spend money on food, I must not forget that I sell books for a living!

I take my purchases back to the flat but decide I am still not ready to set the kitchen in motion, so I venture out again and find a charming little café, combined with a wine shop, on the Île de la Cité. The building is old and the café is cave-like, with little rooms and little tables, all full of happy people, travellers, and locals. I decide to bring out my notepad, order a glass of red wine, and write for a bit while I wait for my *déjeuner*. I delight in a salad of tomato, olives and anchovies, very simple and straightforward. I follow the salad with sausage and lentils with Swiss chard. The food is fine, the service pleasant. After lunch I purchase a bottle of champagne and white burgundy for my cellar.

Tomato, Onion and Anchovy Salad

Use a firm seasonal tomato for this recipe – a Roma works well. You will need only 1 tablespoon of the dressing, but you can keep the remainder in the refrigerator to use again another day.

Serves me

Slice 1 or 2 tomatoes (depending how hungry you are) fairly thin. Place the slices in a pretty design on a plate.

Press 4 Niçoise olives with your hand to loosen the pits. Remove the pits and slice the olives thin. Scatter over the tomato.

To make the dressing, whisk together 4 tablespoons extra virgin olive oil, 2 teaspoons capers, 2 fillets of anchovies chopped fine, 2 tablespoons lemon juice, ½ teaspoon lemon zest and 1½ teaspoons Dijon mustard.

Drizzle 1 tablespoon of the mixture over the tomato and olives.

Braised Sausage and Lentils with Swiss Chard

If you prefer, you may substitute spinach for the Swiss chard. Use 2 hearty handfuls of leaves with stems removed.

Serves me

In a stainless steel fry pan over medium heat, place ½ teaspoon olive oil and ½ teaspoon butter. Add 1 luscious Toulouse sausage, sear on all sides, then remove from pan.

Into the pan put half of a small onion, diced; 1 clove garlic, minced; and ½ teaspoon of your favourite blend of curry powder. Sauté for about 1 minute before adding ¼ cup diced carrot, a sprig of thyme, ¼ cup green lentils, ½ cup dry white wine and 1½ cups vegetable or chicken broth. Bring this mixture to a happy bubble; add the seared sausage into the mix and simmer for 25 minutes until the lentils are tender and the mixture a wee bit saucy.

Cut 3 leaves of Swiss chard into a rough chiffonade, making sure the tough stems have been removed. Stir into the lentil mixture and cook for a few minutes. Add seasonings to taste as you wish. Remove the thyme sprig and serve.

5, February

When I made the decision to spend a month in Paris, I knew I would need to find a flat with a decent kitchen. This task, I discovered, did not prove to be easy. Most people who come to Paris for a week or two, and who prefer the freedom of a flat to a hotel, are content with a microwave and refrigerator. In Paris the "take-out" fare is superb, and if they have come to the city to visit the historic monuments, museums and art galleries, they most likely do not want to take the time to shop for food and prepare it from scratch. But I do, and a more complete kitchen is what I want.

I am not one to explore opportunities on the Internet, but a friend sent me links to a few websites that advertised flats for rent in Paris, and on Christmas night, after a delicious meal with friends and a few too many glasses of champagne, I initiated my search. The next morning, the telephone woke me out of serious slumber and an American voice on the line enthusiastically introduced himself, reminding me that I had e-mailed him the night before. I was startled by this proclamation, and it took my fuzzy brain a moment to connect the dots. My first question was about the kitchen – I must have a fully operational kitchen. I was assured that this was the case, and after a lengthy discussion, I told my new best friend that I would call him the next day after I had looked again at his website and booked my airplane tickets.

My flat is in a building constructed in the eighteenth century, on the Île de la Cité, in the centre of Paris. And, as I am situated looking into the courtyard, it is blissfully quiet. The view from my desk looks onto the roof and steeple at the back end of Notre Dame. The bells begin ringing at 8:00 a.m. and chime on a very regular basis until 9:00 p.m. I decide not to let any other noise, be it from television (which I never watch anyway), radio or CDs interfere with this magical setting. Basically, I have decided to check out of the real world and immerse myself in this fantasy I have concocted. I want to walk, read, write, cook and eat. I want to observe Parisians in their daily habits, and I am hesitant to make too many plans with others that might detract from spontaneous decisions. And, quite frankly, I am exhausted. The autumn months are the busiest of the year in the cookbook world, and with having a full schedule of events plus running two shops, there has been very little time off *pour moi*. After Christmas I made the difficult decision to close my little shop in the Granville Island Public Market. When I opened this satellite store three and a half years ago, I announced to the world that our main shop had given birth to a little one, and she was beautiful. Even though the shop did not live up to expected revenue flow, closing the doors wasn't easy. But now, here I am in Paris ready to decompress, heal some wounds and begin the adventure of fulfilling another dream.

I am ready to cook!

I venture forth on a long walk to a market in the 7th arrondissement on rue de Sax that I remember from a previous visit. I lose my way, naturally, but eventually I arrive at this gastronomic haven, and it does not take long to begin the delightful chore of purchasing the necessary items for my Parisian pantry. The woman at the stall where I buy my oil, spices, salts and mustards is particularly concerned with the honey I have in my hand

and tries her best to explain why it is not the choice for me. She asks other vendors for help, the health inspector who happens to stop by doing his best, but having three people all at once speaking French to me simply results with me giggling hysterically, spending seventy-eight euros and still having no idea why the honey is wrong for me. Forget the song "One Day My Prince Will Come"; I have changed the words, and the dream, to "One Day My French Will Come."

I take my time to visit all the stalls for the perfect chicken leg, rabbit sausage, cheese, fennel, lemons and more. Soon I am loaded down with parcels and I make my way to the taxi stand to return to my flat. It is late in the day, so lunch and dinner become one. I choose the chicken leg, garlic, Niçoise olives and tomatoes to braise into a one-pot wonder. While the concoction is simmering, I compose a hot salad of blood orange, fennel and Parmesan cheese. Dessert is fresh dates, and the wine is white burgundy. Pinch, pinch; I'm really here!

Braised Chicken Leg with Niçoise Olives and Tomatoes

Serves me

In a stainless steel fry pan over medium–high heat, melt ½ tablespoon each of butter and extra virgin olive oil. Add ½ teaspoon espelette salt and swirl around. Place the gorgeous, large chicken leg into the bubbling fat and brown on both sides. Add to the pan 3 cloves of garlic, cut in half with the green germ removed; 10 to 12 cherry tomatoes; 12 Niçoise olives and a splash of dry white wine. When mixture bubbles, reduce heat to low, cover the pan and let simmer for about 20 minutes.

Roast Fennel Salad with Orange Zest and Parmesan

Depending on the size of the fennel bulb you choose, you will need only a part of it. Use a quarter of a large bulb.

The texture of this dish is crunchy. It is prepared as a hot salad, but is also tasty served cold.

Serves me

Remove the zest from an orange, then cut the orange in half and squeeze out the juice. Set zest and juice aside.

Heat oven to 500° F/260° C. Cut fennel bulb into ¼-inch half moons. In a gratin dish, place ½ tablespoon each of butter and extra virgin olive oil. Put the dish in the oven just until the butter melts. Remove dish from oven, layer the fennel, cover with the juice and zest, grind some black pepper over all and return to the oven for 7 minutes. Remove dish and sprinkle 2 tablespoons grated Parmesan cheese over the fennel; return to the oven for 3 to 5 minutes.

Remove the fennel from the hot dish to a serving plate. Garnish with fennel fronds.

6, February

My desire to be ready for spontaneous opportunity is proving effective. It is Friday morning; the telephone rings and I answer to Enrique, a friend from Barcelona. I met Enrique in Beaune, France, a few years ago when I attended Les Trois Glorieuses (the three glorious ones), which is a fundraiser for the Hospices de Beaune, while celebrating *la paulée*, the barrelling of wine from the year's harvest. The auction brings wine lovers and buyers from around the globe. On the last day of the fete we attended La Paulée de Mersault, an elaborate luncheon for seven hundred where each guest is expected to bring a bottle of his or her favourite wine to share with the others. My host for that weekend was of the belief that each person should bring three bottles of wine, so with excellent guidance I made my way to a wine shop to purchase a delectable selection. Enrique was seated next to me at one of the many long tables in the ancient barrelling room. The event started at noon and we left at 7:30 p.m. after sampling fifty-nine wines. Enrique and I had plenty of time to engage in titillating conversation. We met again later that evening as we separately had been invited to attend the tail end of a more intimate *paulée* for fifty guests at the Maison Joseph Drouhin wine cellars.

That was one of the happiest days I had experienced in years; it offered up every wonderful feeling one can imagine from celebrating hard work, sharing offerings with people never before met, making new friends, having intelligent conversation, eating excellent food and, most incredibly, managing to drink all that wine and living to tell the tale. I felt this new friendship with Enrique could have taken an interesting turn that evening, but we were both sharing our hotel rooms and I had given strict instructions to my roommate that I did not ever want to come back to the room and find a do-not-disturb sign on the doorknob, so begrudgingly, I complied with my own decree.

Enrique and I communicate periodically, and we are fond of each other, so I told him before I began my travels that I would be spending the month of February in Paris. Enrique knows Paris well, he travels a lot with his theatre company and, most importantly, he not only loves food but is also a wonderful cook. He is coming to Paris, tonight. Could he stay with me over the weekend? He needs to be in Paris on business the early part of the week, and he would love to show me some of his haunts. I hesitate for a moment; my flat is a one bedroom, but the divan in the sitting room is suitable for sleeping, so I say yes. I am not to expect him until 9:00 p.m. I hang up the telephone and let my nerves take over.

But I have a busy day planned, so I jump into action. I am meeting a friend at her home in the 17th arrondissement, which I observe to be residential and grand. I am ushered into an elegant home that has been stylishly modernized, but I can still visualize the desk in the open lofty room on the second floor where Edmond Rostand wrote *Cyrano de Bergerac*. We chat while nibbling Fauchon gâteau and sipping espresso. A friend of hers joins us for café, and together – frenetically – they help me map my way to the restaurant where I am meeting two Canadians for lunch.

Chris and Jeff are men whose lives I envy. They manage to live, work and support not only themselves but family as well in Paris. Every Friday they meet for lunch at a different eatery, always searching for the perfect meal with entertaining ambiance. Today they have struck gold. This little café, Saint Amour, I would guesstimate seats about thirty patrons. One very eccentric man, who hails from the south of France where he once cooked in a two-star Michelin restaurant, does everything. He cooks, serves the food, pours the wine and does the dishes. And for a little extra cash flow he sells cigarettes. There is one menu each day and very few wines to choose from, so he tends to make that decision for you.

Jeff is a loquacious chap who also is very fond of wine, so our wee gathering soon becomes boisterous. Chris asks me what I have planned for the weekend and his eyebrows rise a little when I admit to having a gentleman visit. Chris is a sensitive man and inquires about my nerves. I giggle, a little.

Soon we are presented with an amazing foie gras terrine. I linger over this dish in an ethereal fog, knowing I will never try to emulate it at home. Our chef clears the empty plates to make room for the next course, which I am excited to receive after such a delightful appetizer. But, I am disappointed with a rather plain piece of salmon, most likely farmed, accompanied with steamed white rice and sautéed green beans. Did I already say you can find bad food in Paris? I allow my thoughts to wander to create a recipe with wild salmon that would make me happier, by simply adding a pat of artichoke butter on a roasted fillet and serving it with a fava bean succotash.

The meal is finished with a delicious tarte tatin made with heirloom apples, though the centre is a little chilly as the tarte was obviously frozen and warmed in a microwave. I decide to finish the menu in my head instead with sautéed apple wedges and Armagnac ice cream.

Wild Salmon Roasted with Artichoke Butter and Fava Bean Succotash

Succotash is a dish I often cook on Thanksgiving or Christmas. But it is not necessarily an autumnal or winter dish. It is really best when your corn is fresh, but good frozen organic corn is a fine substitute.

You can prepare the compound butter ahead of time. If you have a few of these concoctions in your freezer, you can easily and quickly add elegance to a meagre piece of meat, poultry or seafood. For this menu, you can buy canned artichoke hearts, but those bought fresh from your local delicatessen are best.

Fava Bean Succotash

Serves me with leftovers

Have all the ingredients in wee bowls ready to cook: 1 tablespoon butter, 1 clove minced garlic, ¼ cup diced red pepper, 2 tablespoons vegetable stock, ¼ cup fresh fava beans or fresh or frozen edamame, ¼ cup black-eyed peas (rinse the dry peas and then either soak overnight before cooking or simmer for 30 minutes; drain and allow to cool), ¼ cup corn kernels, 1 spring onion sliced fine, 1 teaspoon fresh thyme leaves, a sprinkle of espelette salt, a grind of black pepper and a handful of chopped cilantro leaves.

Melt the butter in a fry pan over medium heat. Add the garlic and red pepper, sautéing them romantically together for a moment. Add the stock, beans, peas, corn and onion; bring to a gentle simmer and cook for about 3 minutes. Season to taste with thyme, salt and pepper. Stir in the cilantro. Add a little more butter for a silken finish. Turn heat to low and set aside.

Artichoke Butter Combine in a food processor ¼ pound unsalted butter (cut it into 4 cubes), 3 artichoke hearts, 1 teaspoon chopped chives, 1 teaspoon lemon zest, 1 teaspoon lemon juice and 2 pinches of Maldon salt. Blend until smooth.

Place mixture on a long piece of plastic wrap. Roll into a log, wrapping it with the plastic wrap. Store the butter log in the freezer until needed.

I think you'll enjoy rolling the butter with plastic wrap. I find this process both fun and sensual at the same time. I actually believe culinary school was my foray into an education about sex!

Roasted Salmon

Serves me with leftover butter

Heat oven to 400° F/200° C and preheat an ovenproof gratin dish. Pour 2 teaspoons extra virgin olive oil and 1 teaspoon lemon citrus salt into a small fry pan. Once these two ingredients are happily bubbling, place a 6-ounce salmon fillet, skin side down, into the pan and cook for a good 2 minutes, long enough to crisp the skin nicely.

In a preheated gratin dish, place the green tops of 6 spring onions (about 4 inches long) and top with ½ teaspoon artichoke butter and 2 tablespoons white wine. Place the salmon, skin side up, on top of the nest of onions and bake for 8 to 10 minutes. When cooked to satisfaction, place the salmon, skin side down, onto the plate of succotash. Cut a piece of artichoke butter from the log, about ½ inch, and place it onto the salmon.

Sautéed Apple Wedges

Choose whatever apple you wish for this simple recipe. A Spartan cohabits nicely with the ice cream. My personal favourite is McIntosh.

Serves me

Peel and core 1 apple and cut into 10 wedges. In a fry pan over medium heat melt together 1 tablespoon butter, 1 tablespoon honey and a good pinch of ground cinnamon. Add the apple pieces, making sure they are well covered with the butter and honey mixture. Lower the heat, cover and simmer for about 15 minutes, or until they are the desired texture, but the colour should be tawny.

Apple Armagnac Ice Cream

Serves me and a few others

Peel and core two Spartan apples and cut into wedges. Place the apples in a fry pan over medium heat and add ¼ cup apple cider, ¼ teaspoon granulated sugar, 1 teaspoon lemon juice and a pinch of salt. Cook until the liquid is absorbed into the apples, about 10 minutes, but do not caramelize. Put the mixture into a bowl and stir until it reaches the consistency of applesauce.

In a pot over medium heat, combine 1 cup whipping cream, ½ cup milk and a small cinnamon stick. Bring to a simmer; remove from heat and cool to room temperature. Remove the cinnamon stick and stir the cream mixture into the applesauce. Stir in 2 tablespoons Armagnac brandy. Cool in freezer for 1 hour before transferring the mixture into an ice cream maker (follow manufacturer's instructions).

When I arrive home much later in the afternoon, after trolling around Paris with Chris for a while, there is a message from Enrique. He has missed his flight and will arrive later than anticipated, by train.

I take myself away from the flat to distract myself at the nearby BHV department store, buying placemats, cloth serviettes and candles.

Around midnight, Enrique arrives; *il est fatigué*. We share some white burgundy and chat for a short while before retiring for the evening to our separate spaces.

7, February

I awake to hear someone rustling in the kitchen. I quickly remember I have a guest, a male guest. I lie in my bed and start to think about the day ahead and wonder what we will do. Enrique knocks lightly on the door of my chamber and, not waiting for a response, he saunters in with breakfast – café, yogurt and segmented grapefruit – serving me in bed. We chat excitedly, making plans for a day centred around food. First stop on our agenda is my local café for espresso and *pain au chocolat*. Actually, I decide to order an Americano with warm milk on the side, which does not meet with anyone's approval, but it is what I want, and in a city that takes pride in fulfilling one's desires, I intend to do as much as I can to accommodate the wishes of the city *and* me.

It has begun to snow. How romantic; snow falling on Paris, you and me. We find the closest metro station and make our way to lunch at a charming bistro on avenue Rapp in the 7th arrondissement. The trip is humorous as Enrique becomes confused about the direction we are to take, and we hop on and off the metro a few times before finally giving up and walking the rest of the way on the snowy streets.

Les Clos de Gourmets is happy to see Enrique; he is a frequent guest at the restaurant. On a previous visit to Paris, I had enjoyed a lovely meal here on his recommendation, but then I was alone. Today, sharing both the experience and the food is very, very pleasant. He chooses a bottle of Tête du Lard to drink with our meal; we select different items so we can share a variety of dishes. We commence with scrambled eggs, salad with beet purée and celery chips. Next is steak tartare with celeriac remoulade, roasted calamari with polenta, and roast chicken and potatoes. Finally, cheese, and then for dessert, Paris-Brest. After espresso, we concur our palates are completely satisfied and decide to digest our meal in the cinema on the Champs-Élysées.

After the film, we flag a taxi to take us to La Grande Épicerie, a very grand food emporium. Enrique is in his element, sashaying through the store, buying as much as we together can carry. What ecstasy, but how will I ever consume all of this food? Another taxi is hailed; we cruise happily through Paris laden with wine and delicious ingredients, ready to prepare a simple and delicate dinner.

We enjoy a few slices of prosciutto, succulent melon, steamed broccoli with black sesame salt, and brie with pears and almonds. We drink a glass or two of Pinot Noir. We are both happy to retire early as the plan for the next day is to rise early, cook a hearty breakfast, explore, then dine out for a late lunch before Enrique leaves me to meet up with his business associates.

Pan-Fried Calamari with Creamy Polenta

When preparing calamari, I follow the advice of one of my favourite New York chefs, Dave Pasternack, owner of Esca and author of the cookbook *Young Man and the Sea*.

Dave says, "Calamari is squid. No matter what they're called and what size they are, calamari have 10 tentacles. Buy the small ones that smell like the ocean. I use the tentacles as well as the head of the squid: Remove the tentacles as one whole piece by slicing off just above where they begin. Slice the body into ½-inch rings. Use your fingers to pull the cartilage out of the head and continue slicing."

Serves me and you

Creamy Polenta
Bring 1 cup of water to a boil in a small saucepan. Add ¼ cup polenta. Whisk constantly until thick. Turn heat down and simmer gently, uncovered, for 15 minutes. Add 1 tablespoon butter, salt and pepper to taste, and ½ cup whipping cream. Set aside.

Pan-Fried Calamari
Prepare 2 small calamari, following Dave Pasternack's instructions (see above). Mix together 1 tablespoon flour, ¼ teaspoon hot smoked paprika and ¼ teaspoon salt. Dredge the calamari through the mixture.

In a fry pan, heat ¼ cup grape seed oil over medium high heat. Shake any excess flour from the calamari, then place in the oil and brown nicely, about 2 minutes.

Serve the calamari on top of the polenta and sprinkle with chopped chives. Add lemon salt or a squeeze of lemon juice.

8, February

Sunday morning and the bells of Notre Dame are celebrating the religious experience; I am lolling in my bed remembering that if my father were still alive, today he would be ninety years of age.

My father was a wonderful cook, although I don't remember, as I was very young when he left our home. It was my Aunt Mary who told me numerous stories of his acumen in the kitchen, and it was not until several years after his passing that I realized what an influence his cooking had been for my (much) older brother and sister. While Mother believed in good ingredients, she was not an inspired cook. Both my brother and sister cook basic food thoughtfully and full of flavour.

Again this morning I hear a rustling in the kitchen, but instead of pretending to be a princess, waiting for my breakfast to be served in my chamber, I jump from my horizontal position because I want to cook with Enrique. We decide to try and emulate the scrambled eggs we enjoyed so much at Les Clos de Gourmets yesterday, and I want to observe what he has in mind and add my two bits.

Well, I realize this is not going to be easy as I observe a masterful display of independence and desire to perform and execute the perfect breakfast for me.

Breakfast is served at the table. Enrique has already been to the *boulangerie* for croissants and he serves them with farm-churned butter and sliced cold ham. Cantaloupe melon has been cubed and put into a bowl with blueberries and a splash of champagne.

The eggs are magnificent; he serves them with sautéed cherry tomatoes. I ask him about the recipe for the scrambled eggs; is it his own? When he tells me his favourite recipe is really one he adapted from Michel Roux, I burst into laughter, telling Enrique that Michel is a friend who recently visited my shop to promote his book *Eggs*. I have impressed Enrique with my cooking friend, and he has impressed me with his cooking.

After our delicious breakfast we hit the streets of Paris. No direction is chosen, and we saunter aimlessly through the 4th arrondissement, looking in windows of shops, expressing our desires for the beautiful objects beyond our grasp. I love this French custom, which we once enjoyed in Canada, of the shops being closed on Sunday. Couples, families and friends are allowed and encouraged to enjoy one another's company. Only food and drink or tourist-related businesses are permitted to open on Sunday.

Scrambled Eggs with Sautéed Cherry Tomatoes

Two dozen cherry tomatoes should be sufficient for 2 servings. If the tomatoes have their stems attached, remove them and give the fruit a jolly good rinse. Clarifying the butter for your fry pan is optional – I am just following Enrique's instructions here.

Serves me and you

Into a medium-size fry pan, pour 1 tablespoon extra virgin olive oil, ½ teaspoon espelette salt and a grind of black pepper. Heat for a minute, then add the tomatoes. When the mixture starts to bubble, turn the heat down and let simmer for about 10 minutes or until the tomatoes are soft and wrinkled.

Break 4 large eggs into a medium-size bowl and beat them lightly with a fork. Brush the bottom of a fry pan with ½ ounce clarified butter. Pour the eggs into the pan and set it over low heat. Stir gently with a wooden spatula until the eggs are creamy. Remove the pan from the heat and season to taste. (Remember that the tomato recipe is highly seasoned, so you won't need to add much salt or pepper to the eggs.)

Divide the eggs between 2 plates. Spread the eggs over the plate, and put the cherry tomato mixture in the middle of the eggs. Sprinkle with finely chopped chives.

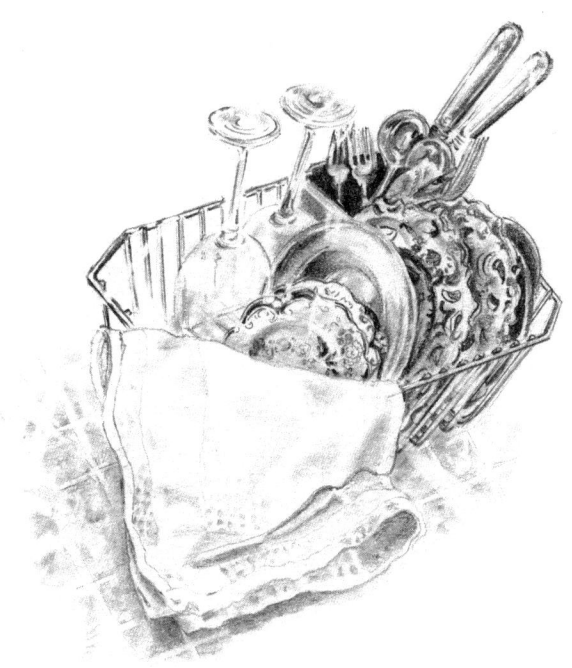

At some point we decide it is time for lunch, so we make our way to Le Dome restaurant. I have long wanted to visit this place, which was made famous in the 1920s when it was frequented by the likes of Ernest Hemingway. It now boasts an exemplary, though somewhat dated, seafood menu. Walking through the door I am instantly transported to another era. The walls are lined with signed photographs of famous visitors. Machismo waiters of a certain age dressed in weathered tuxedos manoeuvre their way through the room. The decor would insult innovative designers of today, but not me. I relax into a banquet, gently shutter my eyelids, ask Enrique to order champagne for me and transport myself to another world, allowing the ambiance to embrace me with its memories.

The champagne arrives; we salute the past and ourselves, and with eyes wide open we choose our meal. Enrique has been to Le Dome before and loves the turbot, exclaiming that it is the only dish he ever orders here. Today, however, he insists that I have the turbot and he chooses the monkfish. When our plates arrive the waiter places the turbot in front of Enrique, who asks for the mistake to be corrected. The maître d' arrives quickly to join the waiter in astonishment, proclaiming this is indeed an occasion, witnessing Enrique forgo the turbot.

After lunch we make our way back to the flat; Enrique collects his luggage to move to a hotel and our visit comes to an end. I am surprised at how much I have enjoyed myself. I pour myself a glass of wine and settle into a comfy chair with a good book. The book I have chosen to bring to Paris is *The Elegance of the Hedgehog* by Muriel Barbery. The story takes place in Paris, so this is going to be another luxury for me: reading a book while I sit in the scene.

9, February

The telephone rings very early. It is Enrique, asking me to hop into a taxi and make my way to his hotel, as he would love me to join him for breakfast before his busy day begins. I do just that. It is a rainy, grey morning, much like I am accustomed to in Vancouver. His hotel is near the Arc de Triomphe, and with the morning traffic, motoring along the avenues takes a while. The slow journey does not trouble me; the city is so generous with its beauty and I love observing Paris waking up.

Enrique and breakfast are waiting, and though the food is not as good as the breakfast he cooked for me yesterday, we are happy to be sharing the moment, laughing together, remembering special moments of the past few days, before we say goodbye for the day.

I decide to enjoy the rain and walk back to my flat. Naturally, this experience with Enrique has left my brain muddled. But I remember Jack Kerouac writing in *Big Sur*, "Why not live for fun and joy?" and am pleased with myself for doing just that.

While I have a map, I am inclined to avoid the most direct routes and enjoy wandering the many streets and avenues. I choose to march down the Champs-Élysées, taking refuge in the Crillon Hotel to catch my breath and dry out. I realize when I finally make it back to the flat that I have been walking for three hours and I am very cold, wet and famished. I have plenty of provisions in my refrigerator from the shopping spree at La Grande Épicerie, but first I luxuriate in a hot bubble bath, pinching myself again, so happy to be free of my world, so far away.

For lunch I compose a salad of baby arugula, avocado, ham and beef tongue with pistachios and cherry tomatoes. Cheese and frozen grapes are the perfect finale.

I spend the afternoon lazing about, reading, writing, napping. For dinner I sauté rabbit sausages with fennel and cherry tomatoes, and serve them with steamed carrots.

I have never understood why some people feel odd about eating rabbit. I love animals, and in my life have enjoyed the companionship of many pets, including a dog, turtle, goldfish, cat, budgie, chicken, rooster, pigeons and, at one time, a garden full of frogs. And throughout my life, during my travels, I have eaten all types of creatures. I embrace the cuisine of the culture I have chosen to explore. And now, in my small corner of the world, we are farming rabbits, to be consumed. So, I implore of you all, please give this delicate hopper a chance and enjoy how your body digests this protein easier than it will red meat. In Paris, rabbit sausages are commonplace. However in Vancouver, you must beg for them, and I often beg Jan van der Lieck, owner of Oyama Sausage Company, to provide me with his delicious recipe. I know he will have them in his shop regularly if more of us become adventurous in our culinary desires.

Rabbit Sausages with Fennel and Cherry Tomatoes

For a meal for myself I will eat five sausages. Do not think me a glutton; these sausages are small – the size of breakfast sausages. Serve them with a vegetable of your choice, such as steamed broccoli or carrots, for a lovely accompaniment.

Serves me

In a fry pan, melt 1 tablespoon olive oil and 1 teaspoon butter. Sear the sausages on all sides until just brown; remove from pan. Add to the pan ½ cup finely sliced fennel and 8 to 10 cherry tomatoes. Once mixture is bubbling, return the sausages to the pan. Cover and simmer on low heat for about 10 minutes.

Stir 10 leaves of fresh tarragon into the sauce and season with salt and pepper. Turn off the heat and add 1 tablespoon cold butter for an elegant finish.

10, FEBRUARY

After a visit to my café, Le Lutétia, that I enjoy so much every morning, I return to the flat for a few hours of reading *Hedgehog*. I love this book, and though it is hard to put it down, I must, as I am entertaining tonight.

On my last visit to Paris, I met a woman, Rachel, through mutual friends. We enjoyed each other's company, so I have invited her for dinner. Rachel is from Vancouver. She met a French man fifteen years ago, married him, gave birth to a son, and is now going through a messy divorce that will most likely result in her leaving Paris and returning to Canada to live. The flat she lives in is beautiful; it will be difficult for her to give it up. I feel horribly sad for her and am determined to cheer her up with a nice dinner.

I mosey around the shops, wondering what she might like to eat. I am not feeling overly creative, which is odd considering the display of beauty I see spread before me in *la boucherie*, so I play it safe and choose loin of pork. One of my standard meals for one or two people is roast loin of pork with shitake mushroom sauce and cranberry compote. I often have cranberry compote in the freezer in small packets so I can easily warm it up with a bit of cognac to accompany the pork. I like to serve this combination with a tian of orange sweet potatoes and sautéed spinach. But today, I can't find cranberries or orange sweet potatoes, so I change thoughts and decide to roast the pork loin and serve it with an apple cider sauce. I will slice some carrots and leeks into coin-size rounds and then steam them. For dessert, I plan a recipe of ginger poached pears.

I make an artichoke dip to enjoy with our champagne. I haven't made this artichoke dip for years. When I had my restaurant, this dip was presented to guests in a little ramekin with melba toast soon after they settled at their table. Everyone seemed to love it, and it was so simple to prepare.

I predict we will chat our way through the bottle of champagne before dinner and desire a bottle of Pinot Noir for our meal. Am I bothered about a fuzzy head in the morning? *Mais non*, I am at liberty.

When Rachel arrives, she immediately spots the book I am reading and exclaims excitedly that she too is reading *The Elegance of the Hedgehog*, in French of course, and loving it.

During dinner the telephone rings; it is Pat, the woman I am going to meet later in the week for drinks. We chat for a moment before I mention that I have a friend dining with me, so I must sign off. When I return to the table I mention to Rachel that I will be meeting this woman, Pat, who has a husband called Bernard and that they are friends of a great pal in Vancouver. Rachel starts to reminisce fondly about a woman she knew years ago in Paris called Pat with a husband named Bernard. Although I quickly realize this is indeed the same couple, I let her rattle on for a bit before informing her of this fact. It was good to hear her speak of her early days and happier times in Paris.

Artichoke Dip

You can make the mayonnaise ahead of time and refrigerate it until you are ready to make this dip. Homemade mayonnaise is best eaten within a day or two of making. Leftover mayonnaise pairs beautifully with almost any type of fish or meat or with steamed or raw vegetables and salads. I also use it with Watercress Salad with Crab.

Serves me and you

To prepare lemon chive mayonnaise, in a bowl whisk until smooth 1 egg yolk, zest of half a lemon, 1 tablespoon lemon juice, 1 teaspoon Dijon mustard and a pinch each of salt and pepper. Continue to whisk while adding ¾ cup extra virgin olive oil, very gradually, allowing the mixture to thicken. Stir in 1 tablespoon chopped chives. Set aside.

In a food processor, coarsely chop 3 artichoke hearts. Add ½ cup of the lemon chive mayonnaise, ¼ cup grated Parmesan cheese and 2 drops truffle oil (optional). Process until smooth.

Divide mixture between 2 half-cup ramekins and bake in a 500° F/260° C oven for 5 minutes.

Serve with your favourite crackers or flatbread.

Roast Pork Tenderloin with Apple Cider Sauce

Choose a crisp, sweet apple for this recipe; I particularly like Fuji apples. If the apple is large, use just half as you do not want the wedges to be too big. I like to serve this dish with steamed leeks and carrots, but you can add whatever vegetables you like.

Serves me and you

Trim fat and sinew from 1 pound of pork tenderloin. Cut in half and set aside.

Heat oven to 475° F/240° C. In a stainless steel fry pan over medium heat, melt together ½ tablespoon each of grape seed oil and butter. To the bubbling fat add 2 teaspoons ground cardamom, ¼ teaspoon salt and 3 grinds of black pepper. Mix together, then add the pork, turning to sear on all sides and covering with the spice mixture.

Peel and core apple and cut into 10 wedges. Place the wedges in the fry pan with the pork, rolling them around with the fat and spices. Put the pan into the hot oven for 10 minutes.

Remove the pork from the pan and let it rest. Return the pan with the apples to the stovetop over medium heat and add ¼ cup vegetable stock and ⅓ cup apple cider; reduce liquid by half. Remove from heat and whisk in 1 tablespoon cold butter.

Slice the pork, place on a serving plate and pour the apple cider sauce over top.

Ginger Poached Pears with Coffee Cream and Ginger Cookies

This recipe is inspired by a dessert that I didn't actually enjoy, served to me at a restaurant on the Île Saint Louis. It reminded me of when

I first fell in love with cooking; I would take my mother's recipes and try to make them better. The name of the restaurant translates to "My Old Friend."

When I prepare this dish, I like to use ginger cookies made from a recipe called Orange Molasses Cookies from *The Special Cookbook* by Mary Patterson. If you want the recipe, you must buy the book!

Serves me and you

In a small saucepan over medium heat, combine 1½ cups each of sugar and water. Bring to a simmer; let the sugar dissolve completely. Slit open a vanilla bean and remove the seeds. To the sugar mixture, add ¼ of the bean pod and the seeds, along with a 1-inch piece of gingerroot and 1 clove. Let the sugar syrup infuse while preparing the pears.

Peel 2 small Bartlett pears and, with a melon baller, remove the core, working from the bottom and carving into the centre of the pear. Place the pears in the gently simmering syrup. Place a piece of parchment paper or a saucepan lid (smaller than the saucepan you are using) over top to keep the pears submerged.

The time needed to poach the pears will depend on their ripeness. Test them after 8 minutes by lifting one gently from the syrup and poking with a small knife. The pear is done when the knife meets no resistance. If not done, place back into the syrup and check again in 3 minutes. Remove pears to a bowl, pouring the syrup over top, straining out the clove, ginger and vanilla pod. Let cool to room temperature.

To make the coffee cream, stir together ½ cup whipping cream and $\frac{1}{8}$ teaspoon natural coffee extract. Whisk the mixture into soft peaks.

Crumble 2 ginger cookies. Place each pear on a plate and sprinkle with the crushed cookies. Place a dollop of coffee cream beside each pear and serve.

11, FEBRUARY

Tonight I am dining with my landlord, Glenn Cooper. When I first arrived in Paris, Glenn was not here to meet me as he was off skiing in Switzerland, but he had one of his staff take me to the flat and help me settle in. I am full of intrigue about Glenn; we have had such delightful chats on the telephone. This intrigue is not romantically inspired as I am pretty sure he "goes to a different church," but I am always curious about how people from North America have managed to make their lives work in Paris. Originally from New York, Glenn has been living in Paris for the past fifteen years and sounds, to me, to be a very happy man.

He has a favour to ask; could he please come early with a carpenter in tow? He has plans to renovate the flat after I depart. I am already so attached to this place; I don't want him to do a thing to change it. Once they are here, I enjoy their banter, but I am happy to see the carpenter leave so I can open some wine and get to know Glenn. Of course, I had hoped Glenn had reserved a table at some tony restaurant for dinner. Instead, he wants to discuss at length where we should dine. He appears to be quite worried about my dining habits as he is much more of an "eat to live" kind of a guy and, he tells me, since he eats out every day, neither he nor his partner ever cook for themselves or each other. Plus, the cost of food is an issue.

After too much wine (again) and no decision on where to eat, I demand he take me to his favourite restaurant on the Île de la Cité. A nice bonus is the short walk to our destination, where we are received at the restaurant with great enthusiasm. Imagine a British comedy show from the 1960s where the French restaurant is typified as a bordello with red-tufted silk draping from the ceiling. Complete the image with flamboyant service and classic French cuisine.

For my meal, I order duck with orange sauce; Glenn orders the roast chicken. The maître d' places before us kir royale served in a ruby red coupe and large plates of little fried pan crêpes that are thick morsels with a lacy edging.

This clichéd dining experience provides great entertainment for me. I love Paris.

Roast Chicken with Orange Sauce

This recipe brings back the memories of Glenn's chicken and my duck. Whenever you can, buy the best chicken available. If you are lucky enough to be in Paris, this is easy to do, as poor-quality chicken is hard to find. When I am cooking this dish for myself, I purchase one large chicken leg. Serve with a salad made with greens and walnuts.

Serves me

Heat the oven to 475° F/240° C. In a stainless steel fry pan, splash in some oil and 1 tablespoon of butter. Rub salt and pepper onto a chicken leg, place in the hot fry pan and sear each side. Put the pan with the chicken into the hot oven for about 13 to 15 minutes.

Remove the chicken from the pan onto a plate, draining the oil but leaving the bits in the pan. Remove zest from 1 orange; peel and segment the fruit. Set aside. Juice a second orange. Pour ¼ cup dry white wine into the pan with the orange juice. Reduce the liquid while scraping all the bits together. Add both orange zest and segments to the pan. Salt and pepper to taste. Remove pan from heat and whisk in 1 tablespoon cold butter. Pour sauce over chicken and serve.

Endive, Watercress, Frisée and Walnut Salad with Walnut Oil and Sherry Vinaigrette

I have always loved walnuts, but since this trip to Paris, walnuts make me giggle. Enrique and I were shopping at the market one day and came home with a bag of fresh walnuts in the shell. The flat did not have a nutcracker so Enrique proceeded to crack them open in his hands. I found this act of masculine bravura rather sensual, which of course enticed Enrique to open them all in this manner.

Serves me

Slice about 5 endive leaves into 3 pieces each. Toss with 1 small handful of watercress and 1 small handful of frisée, washed and picked over. Add 8 walnuts, roughly chopped.

Whisk together 1 tablespoon each of walnut oil and sherry vinegar in a bowl. Drizzle over salad. Finish with a pinch of orange salt.

12, February

My morning starts, as usual, at Le Lutétia. I love this French custom. Actually, I do have a café in Vancouver that I frequent for coffee most mornings called Uva. And I love it, too. But in this café in Paris, I write and observe, while at home I do what everyone else is doing here, which is chat.

As a young girl, I could usually be found reading a book or writing poetry. It was not good poetry, but I loved pretending I could write. As I became a young woman, I lost the patience to hone this craft and let the desire to become a writer be erased from my thoughts.

Much later, around the time I was celebrating a significant birthday, I was introduced to John, who helped me rekindle my desire to write. John is a man who has a unique talent for writing beautifully, observing the human race from a particular perspective, while knowing how to make an openhearted soul feel incredibly special. He came into my life when I was trying, with difficultly, to realize two dreams – write a cookbook and open my cookbook shop – and I was determined to keep both ideas close to my chest. But I did open up to John, and he immediately decided to become a cheerleader. He joined my great pal Veryl (a wonderful woman who lived a long, good life but died while her spirit was youthful) and Danny, my fish-man friend, to form a triumvirate that guided me on a daily basis to ensure my dreams came true. John also took on the role of mentoring me to write, and a romantic attachment ensued. Lucky for me, John is still in my life, still encouraging me to write, and still offering words of wisdom.

And now, I am in Paris, once again writing, and enjoying every moment of it.

Rachel has telephoned and asked me to meet her at E. Dehillerin. She needs a lid for a copper pot, and I have never been to the renowned cookware shop so I'm happy to come along and gawk. The shop was established in 1820 and I doubt there have been many changes to the decor since it opened. It is a healthy walk from my flat, but enjoyable. I arrive early; Rachel arrives late, with dog in tow. This custom of dogs accompanying their owners wherever they go used to amuse me, but I now find the relationships people have with their pets a touch tedious. I guess, really, I don't like competing for the attention. We spend quite a while in the shop; my purchase comprises an asparagus server, a tart server and an olive scoop. Rachel finds her copper lid and we head off for café au lait and croissants, and on the way she gives me a tour of some of the marvellous buildings in the area.

After we part, I head back to my neighbourhood and make a stop at the bookshop Shakespeare and Company. I want a cookbook, no particular title, because I am finding it difficult to live in a home without one. I should have gone to Librairie Gourmande to make this purchase; I was so close when I was at Dehillerin. But, I was not thinking clearly, a trait I am becoming used to with all this freedom, and anyway, I am in the mood for something eccentric.

On the shelf, among an exceptionally paltry cookbook selection, I find a previously enjoyed Scottish cookbook by Clare Macdonald, and I am delighted with it. I head home with high hopes of inspiring ideas eager to leap off the pages into my brain. I make a cup of tea and sit down with my prize. I don't find even one recipe that I want to cook, but then, cookbooks are written to inspire and this one stirs a memory of a dish that I have cooked successfully before and want to make now: crab and turnip gratin with cloves. And wouldn't it be lovely with a smoked salmon and frisée salad with mustard lemon vinaigrette? So back I go to the shops to buy the ingredients. When I have finished this late lunch, I head out to the *pâtisserie* for a chocolate éclair, bringing it home to enjoy with tea while reading *Hedgehog*.

Crab and Turnip Gratin

I like to do as much one-pot cooking as possible, and this recipe fits the bill. A 7-inch stainless steel pan works well for this dish. If you wish, you can replace the crabmeat with duck confit. Purchase 1 duck leg and cook it in a fry pan over medium heat to melt the fat away. Turn the leg often to get the fat off efficiently; you do not want to cook the duck. Once all the fat is removed, strip the bone of its meat and shred it to use in this recipe.

Serves me (with leftovers)

Peel a medium-size turnip (about 4 inches round) and boil it whole for about 12 minutes. Cool before dicing into ½-inch cubes. Set aside.

In a medium-size pan, melt 1 tablespoon butter over medium-high heat. Add 2 tablespoons grated onion and ⅛ teaspoon ground cloves. Let the mixture bubble away for about 2 minutes.

Add ½ cup heavy cream; reduce slightly. Add ¼ cup grated Parmesan cheese, salt and pepper to taste. Fold half of the cubed turnip into the creamy mixture. Top this first with ¼ cup fresh crabmeat, the rest of the turnip, and another ¼ cup crabmeat. Sprinkle ½ cup grated Parmesan cheese over all and cook in a hot oven, 375° F/190° C, for about 20 minutes until browned and bubbly.

Smoked Salmon and Frisée Salad with Mustard Lemon Vinaigrette

Serves me

To make vinaigrette, whisk together 1 teaspoon Dijon mustard, 1 tablespoon lemon juice, 1 teaspoon lemon zest and a pinch each of salt and pepper. Gradually whisk in ¼ cup extra virgin olive oil. Toss 1 good-size handful of frisée with the dressing. Serve onto a plate over 2 to 3 thin slices of smoked salmon.

13, February

Today is my brother's birthday. I wonder if he ever wanted to visit Paris. This will be the first year of my life that I do not try to connect with him and give him best wishes on his special day. Well, it certainly was my father's special day, welcoming a son into his life. I feel sad about all of these remembrances. Since my mother died four years ago, my brother and I have spoken only three times. I guess it could be compared to a divorce provoked and completed by just one of the duo in question. Only very recently have I accepted the fact that our relationship has ended, and I have adjusted my life to living without my brother.

But not all thoughts of my brother are sad. He has two wonderful children who do not live near me, but with whom I've maintained a loving relationship. I once had a secret dream that Dylan and Lana would embrace the world of food and want to take over my bookshop one day. I am satisfied with the knowledge they both love to eat and cook for themselves. For Lana's fourteenth birthday I gifted her with a personalized copy of Mark Bittman's *How to Cook Everything*. And on one of Dylan's birthdays I invited him into my shop and extended liberty to pick out any cookbook his heart desired. Well, I am not sure if it was his heart that guided him, but his desire focused on a book with a poster perfect picture of Nigella Lawson.

When Lana turned sixteen, I took her to New York and gave her just two rules: no to fast food and yes to sampling all of the exotic fare presented on the many plates set before her. She proved to be a magnificent dining companion. I took her to the James Beard Awards, hosted by some of the finest restaurants and chefs in the world, and she was in a trance. She became entirely enchanted with Bob Blumer, spending most of her time hanging about his table; she managed to bring his name into the conversation for days to come. I would wager well that Blumer would pay attention to her mature beauty now! And when Dylan turned sixteen, I treated him to the same journey with the same rules. However, Dylan did manage to convince me that a hotdog outside the Metropolitan Museum of Art should not be considered fast food but an integral part of New York culture. When I took Dylan to the James Beard Awards, he fell in love with Emily Luchetti and cheered loudest when she was awarded Pastry Chef of the Year. Maybe one day we'll all be in Paris together.

But, as my granny would say, if wishes were horses, beggars would ride. And lucky me, I AM IN PARIS, and tonight I am meeting two women for drinks in the 6th arrondissement at le café les éditeurs, a stylish bar noted for attracting literary types. Pat is a Canadian woman who came to Paris many years ago after the death of her first husband and was most fortunate to meet a wonderful man, Bernard; she never returned to Canada to live, only to visit. We have a mutual friend, Richard, in Vancouver who insisted upon our meeting, and so Pat has organized today's outing.

I am given explicit instructions to take the metro, told where to depart, and that I will be met at the top of the stairs. I arrive early and observe the many lovers embracing and kissing as they meet or depart from one another. Michelle, a friend of Pat's, originally from Montreal, identifies me. We are soon joined by Pat and instantly form a comfortable threesome. Michelle tours us around some of her favourite shops in the neighbourhood, pointing out the best places to buy chocolate and shoes, and showing us the Village Voice Book Shop. I'm sure you can visualize this picture.

When we find the perfect table at les éditeurs, we choose a bottle of Sancerre and begin to discover just how many people we know in common. And of course, they are wonderfully generous with ideas of things for me to do to experience the best of Paris.

We finish our wine; it is about 7:00 p.m. and we say goodbye. I look forward to seeing Pat again on the twenty-first, when she has invited me to her home for lunch. Even though I am now metro savvy, I decide to walk home, thinking about what I will prepare for myself for dinner. A simple duck confit hash comes to mind.

Sweet Potato and Duck Confit Hash

Having a leg of duck confit in your refrigerator is a blessing when you crave this simple dish.

Serves me

To remove fat from the duck leg, place the leg in a fry pan over medium heat. Turn the leg several times until the fat has melted away from the meat. Leave the fat in the pan, and remove the leg. Shred the duck meat and set aside.

Heat oven to 375° F/190° C. Cut 1 smallish orange sweet potato into ½-inch cubes and put into pan with the duck fat. Add a grind or two of black pepper.

Place the pan in the hot oven for about 20 minutes. Test the sweet potato with a fork (it should be soft). Remove from the oven and combine with the shredded duck. Cover and set aside while you prepare the egg.

To poach the egg, start with fresh, cold water. Bring to a simmer in a shallow pan. Add 1 teaspoon of apple cider vinegar. Crack the egg into a shallow bowl, then slide it into the simmering water. Cook to desired doneness.

Meanwhile, take a hearty handful of baby arugula and mix into the sweet potato and duck mixture. Place on your serving plate, and with a slotted spoon remove the poached egg from its bath and place on top of the hash.

14, FEBRUARY

I cannot pretend to be enthusiastic about spending Saint Valentine's Day, the sacred day of love, alone in Paris. I am content though, with the knowledge that I have many people in my life who love me, and maybe even one or two who could be happy spending this day *avec moi*. That being said, the day has been special for me. The weather is particularly glorious. I commence my walk away from the 4th arrondissement, heading up the Seine into the 7th arrondissement, breaking my journey at Le Café des Beaux Arts for a café crème. I continue my leisurely walk allowing the shop windows to draw me into their world, delighting my senses with paintings, books, haute couture and antiquities.

I stroll down rue du Bac, specifically looking for a shop I remember from a previous visit. Of course some of the items I remember wishing I had bought are no longer available, but I find a few treasures for loved ones at home. I continue on to Café Varenne for café long. While sitting outside, enjoying my café, I notice a shop selling hosiery and excitedly cross the road hoping to indulge this off-beat enthusiasm I have for silly stockings.

Gaya par Pierre Gagnaire, a temple of gastronomie, is where I choose to dine. The room is small and casual; the staff is caring and suitably attentive to a woman dining on her own. I propose a glass of champagne rosé, the perfect enhancement for a happy mood. The menu takes me to that other place, the one where my stomach sends out sensual signals to my mind and I care only about ethereal morsels caressing my palate. I order modestly, my Canadian upbringing clinging closely to the Scottish

side of my gut. I love what I eat: *darn de lieu jaune pochée au beurre, purée de cresson, croquettes de potmarron*. For dessert I choose *crumble de pommes clocharde* and *crème glacée caramel et sirop cidre*.

The walk back to the flat is, naturally, more joyful. I try to walk quickly past a shop displaying beautiful clothes in the windows, but am uncontrollably sucked in, where I ponder wistfully over a pair of jeans priced at 337 euros. Knocking my brain back into place I depart and sally forth to Shakespeare and Company where I make a sensible purchase of love poems and letters by Robert Browning and Elizabeth Barrett Browning.

My evening is a gentle one complete with reading and cooking. I enjoy a simple dinner of chicken livers sautéed in butter and rosé wine with crispy shallots, accompanying a salad of blood oranges with red romaine lettuce and ruby beets.

Just before I retire, the telephone rings; it is Enrique. Saint Valentine's wishes are extended and he advises he will be back in Paris on Wednesday.

My dreams are sweet, and today love is beautiful.

∾

Chicken Livers with Crispy Shallots

A mandoline is a useful kitchen tool to have on hand. I like to use it for slicing the shallots in this recipe.

Serves me

Crispy Shallots

Thinly slice ½ cup shallots. In a fry pan, heat ¼ cup extra virgin olive oil over medium heat and add 3 pinches (about ¼ teaspoon) of espelette pepper. Gently fry for about 7 minutes until the shallots are auburn in colour. Remove and set aside.

Chicken Livers

Cut ¼ pound of chicken livers into about 7 or 8 evenly sized pieces. In the fry pan, heat 2½ teaspoons grape seed oil and ½ teaspoon butter over medium heat. Add a jolly good pinch of espelette salt and a grind of black pepper. Turn the heat up to high, add the chicken liver pieces and sauté each side until nicely browned. Add ¼ cup of rosé wine to the pan (or a splash from your glass) and turn the heat down to low. Simmer for 1 minute.

Remove chicken livers from the pan and turn onto a plate. Add 1 teaspoon butter to the pan to make a sauce; pour over the liver. Top with the crispy shallots and another jolly good grind of pepper.

15, FEBRUARY

The bells of Notre Dame encourage me to jump out of bed for two reasons. I slept well, waking up to the memory of my telephone conversation with Enrique last night, informing me he will be coming to visit on Wednesday, which has my heart racing – a little. And Glenn, my landlord, has invited me to join him on an excursion in the country to troll around a few *brocantes*. In Canada we call them flea markets. In Paris, there are three classes of flea markets, and today we are going middle class.

Glenn lives close to the Louvre, so I am happy to walk my way to meet him at his flat. He is standing on the street outside the building as I approach. "You can't come in, my house is a mess," he states. So we walk into the café on the corner for cappuccinos and croissants while we wait for his partner, Jean-François, and another friend to join us. He warns me that his partner gets very grumpy about these excursions that Glenn likes to make frequently.

Soon we are out of the city, driving into the country. And as predicted, as we travel along, Jean-François whines about the distance we are driving, asking why he is having to do this again. But at the same time it is obvious how fond the two men are of each other, and I enjoy observing Jean-François compromising his own desire to participate in Glenn's passion.

I am excited to be on this little adventure. Glenn is a charming tour guide, and this trio are young, hip and have interesting careers, which I am really happy to be hearing about. I spend so much time in my own world of food and books that I tend to forget people could actually have other interests, or that it just might take a little more to make the world go round than what my "foodie religion" preaches.

After driving for about an hour, Glenn stops for gas. He runs in to pay the bill and comes out with a bag of "treats." I can barely hide my disgust when I witness them enjoying packaged *pain au chocolat*, big bags of candy, Coca-Cola, etc. I prudishly decline any offerings that come my way. I pout for a few minutes, pinch myself to be mindful of what I am doing, and do not allow this display of "fake food gorging" lessen my happy mood.

We arrive at the first of two *brocantes* we will visit. Glenn is ecstatic with the display of treasures, rows and rows of "one man's junk, another man's treasure." We pair off since four people are never going to agree on anything. Soon we are all on our own, but eventually we meet up at the catering truck where we decide it is time to eat lunch. I am worried, but the three men assure me that here are the best sausages to be found in these parts. And they are right. A Toulouse sausage on the perfect baguette with Dijon mustard is presented to me, and it is delicious. I hear a collective sigh of relief from all three of them when I smile widely after my first bite.

After lunch I find some darling little cocktail napkins, pale yellow with a hand-stitched thin white border and a little white leaf embroidered in the corner. I buy all twelve for seven euros. Then I find a very old case containing twelve bone-handled knives for twelve euros. These knives need a bit of work, but I love them. Usually, I am not one to look for deals, but when an item appears to have an interesting history, I take great pleasure in bartering my way into its life.

The day is long, but lovely. While we drive back into the city, I try my best to influence my new friends to eat better food, to cook for themselves and for each other. They are astonished to hear that I will be cooking dinner for myself that night — that I'm actually excited to be cooking just for me, in Paris.

Back home I pour the now customary glass of wine and open the fridge to ponder my evening meal.

I make a roquefort and red pepper butter to melt into a pan-roasted rib-eye steak. I steam green beans and scatter some almonds over the vegetables for good health.

I sit at my table with a full glass of Bordeaux, napkin on my lap, candles flickering, enjoying this simple meal. And the thoughts floating through my head are rather marvellous.

Pan-Roasted Rib-Eye Steak with Roquefort and Red Pepper Butter

My preference for a steak is a rib-eye, about 6 ounces for one person. If you can't find one this size, you have the option of purchasing a small cut of strip-loin or cutting a larger rib-eye steak in half and freezing the extra piece for another occasion. Or, pick up the telephone and invite some deserving friend for a tasty meal.

The compound butter used in this recipe is a favourite of mine from the time I had my restaurant. One of my customers was so enamoured with this colourful butter that he surprised me one day with a present. I unwrapped the gift at the bar when the restaurant was very crowded, discovering a red silk negligee inside. My staff deserted me for the dish pit to laugh hysterically, leaving me alone with a *très rouge* face!

Serves me with leftover butter

Roquefort and Red Pepper Butter To prepare the roquefort and red pepper butter, heat oven to 400° F/200° C. Cut 1 large red pepper in half, remove seeds, and place on baking sheet. Roast for 30 minutes.

Peel the charred skin off the pepper and cut into chunks. Place in a food processor with ¼ pound butter (cut into 4 pieces) and ¼ pound crumbled roquefort cheese. Mix until smooth. Remove the mixture from the processor and place on a piece of plastic wrap on the counter. Form into a log; wrap and freeze until needed.

Pan-Roasted Rib-Eye Steak

To prepare the steak, place a fry pan over medium-high heat. Heat 2 teaspoons extra virgin olive oil to a gentle bubble. Rub 1 teaspoon espelette salt and a grind of black pepper onto both sides of the steak and add to the hot pan. Sear the first side for about 1 minute or until the meat releases its grip and refuses to stick to the pan. Flip the steak over and sear on the second side for about 30 seconds. Place the pan with the steak into heated oven, 400° F/200° C, and roast for 5 to 7 minutes, depending on thickness and desired doneness.

When meat is done, remove steak from the pan to a plate. Cut a round of the prepared butter, about ½-inch thick, and place it on top of the hot meat.

Steamed Green Beans with Toasted Almonds

Allow about 9 green beans per person. Place beans in a steamer over a pan of 1 cup water and a layer of thin slices of lemon. Steam for about 4 minutes. Drain and pair the beans with the steak on a plate. Sprinkle each serving with 1 tablespoon toasted slivered almonds.

16, February

If you are of a certain vintage, a song that will resonate with you is one written and performed by the Beatles, "When I'm Sixty-Four." It is on this day that Danny, my wonderful friend who died four years ago, would have been sixty-four. I lie in my Parisian bed, listening to the bells tolling my remembrances. If Danny were still in the mortal world, what would he have thought of my journey to Paris? I know that if he were here with me, we would be eating in every fishy restaurant the city provided, visiting every fishmonger, and finding every establishment that served salmon from British Columbia. While he would be interested in farmed salmon as well, I would be adamant that only wild fish would be allowed on my plate. We often debated the merits of fresh versus farmed fish, mostly over leisurely dinners of seafood, and I am happy to report that before he left us, the arguments subsided into his acceptance of my convictions.

I decide to dedicate the day to Danny's memory and do things I know he would have liked to do. He defined a luxurious morning as one that began by opening his eyes, reaching for the book he was favouring at the moment and reading in bed. So even though I don't believe in reading in bed (beds are for sleeping and sex), I scurry to the sitting room and grab *Hedgehog* and jump back under the covers to devour the pages. Next on the agenda is to stroll to the café to plan my menu for the day. I leave the café with a list of desires to procure, stopping for a while by the river. Danny loved boats and though within his business he had many boats, for his personal pleasure he spent many happy hours with a grand leisure craft. So, I spend some time on the banks of the Seine to admire the boats sailing by. I really should buy a ticket for one these excursions that so many tourists appear to enjoy. But for now I choose to gaze from the sidelines. I make my way to the fishmonger to purchase enough seafood for a feast. I wonder if I should invite a guest for dinner, but decide I will be happiest not to share these melancholy moments, feeling I will better savour the memories on my own.

I spend a lot of time admiring the fish, remembering our ritual in the kitchen. If a fish needed to be cleaned or filleted, Danny would do that, then retire to a comfortable chair with a glass of wine to observe me cooking the meal. My kitchen at home is designed to accommodate three actions: cooking, chatting and drinking. Of course, being committed to this scenario means that preparing a meal tends to take a while and most often, between the cooking and the time at the table enjoying the meal, the evening is complete.

Being that I am on my own today, I choose crab to make a salad with watercress, tomato and pancetta, clams to steam with white wine, shallots and parsley, and when the clams open their shells to me I dip them in butter melted with garlic and chives. I then dust a fillet of sole with flour and citron salt and pan-fry it until golden. I sauté some asparagus for an accompaniment.

I love everything about this afternoon and evening: the shopping for my supper, cooking slowly and thoughtfully, sitting down to my table with an expensive white wine. It is while enjoying my dinner I think how interesting it is that I have chosen February to travel to Paris for this reflective peace, realizing my father, brother and Danny all have birthdays in February.

It is here I have come to understand my relationships with these men in a way that I had not allowed myself to previously. I think I needed to remove myself from my day-to-day life for a period of time to properly adjust.

After dinner I decide I want to finish reading *Hedgehog*. I am not at all prepared for the ending and I cry uncontrollably. But before I retire, I wash up the kitchen, soak in a hot bath and find myself at peace with my thoughts, prepared to fall in love with the possibilities ahead.

Thank you Danny. Today, I feel you are taking care of me.

Watercress Salad with Crab, Tomato, Pancetta and Lemon Chive Mayonnaise

You will need only 1 to 2 tablespoons of the lemon chive mayonnaise for this salad. Cover and store the remainder in the refrigerator. Use as much or as little of fresh crabmeat as you like – or can afford – in this salad. I prefer to use five shapely legs.

Serves me

To prepare lemon chive mayonnaise, in a bowl whisk until smooth 1 egg yolk, zest of half a lemon, 1 tablespoon lemon juice, 1 teaspoon Dijon mustard and a pinch each of salt and pepper. Continue to whisk while adding ¾ cup extra virgin olive oil, very gradually, allowing the mixture to thicken. Stir in 1 tablespoon chopped chives. Set aside.

Cook 1 slice of pancetta on a baking pan in a 400° F/200° C oven for 8 to 10 minutes, or on the stovetop in a fry pan until crispy. Cool and crumble into small pieces. Dice 1 Roma tomato.

Wash and pick through 1 hearty handful of watercress. Place watercress and crab in a bowl and toss with the prepared mayonnaise. Turn salad onto a serving plate and top with diced tomato and crumbled pancetta.

Steamed Clams with Garlic Butter

Serves me

Rinse 1 pound of clams and put them into a pot with ¼ cup white wine, 1 sliced garlic clove, 1 sliced shallot, 2 tablespoons chopped parsley and a grind of black pepper. Bring the mixture to a boil; cover and steam for about 2 minutes or until all the clams have opened their shells. Remove clams from the pan and place into a serving bowl.

In another pan, melt 3 tablespoons butter mixed with 1 clove finely minced garlic, a squeeze of lemon juice and a pinch of lemon salt. If desired, add some finely chopped chives. Cook together over low heat for 2 minutes. Pour butter into a small dish and dip away.

Pan-Fried Fillet of Sole with Sautéed Asparagus

Serves me

In a fry pan over medium-high heat, melt together 1 teaspoon vegetable oil, 1 teaspoon butter and 1 good pinch espelette salt. Dust 1 fresh fillet of sole, not too thin, with flour and citrus salt. Place in pan and cook for 1 minute. Turn over and cook for another 1 or 2 minutes.

Remove to a warm serving plate. (You can place plate in an oven that has been heated to warm and then turned off.) In the same fry pan, place about 7 asparagus spears, juice of half a lemon, pinch of lemon zest, salt and pepper to taste. Add more butter if needed to sauté the asparagus for a few minutes. Serve with the sole.

17, February

It is hard for the staff at my shop back home to imagine I have been in Paris for fourteen days and not made a visit to Librairie Gourmande, so this is my plan for the morning. I take my time to organize myself for this excursion, not that I feel I need to be overly fashionable before presenting myself to the competition, but I am determined to make an impression, and as that certainly won't happen with my ability to converse in French, I want to look smart.

I have been to this shop before and am very happy to return. I'm also anxious to discover what new and interesting books are on the shelves.

The shop is on two floors. When you enter from the street, you find a woman behind a counter in the middle of the space, though there is a wall behind her. She smiles and quietly says *bonjour*. On the ground floor in the back is a section for the old and out-of-print books, some locked away in a case. These books are all in French. The area directly in front of this antiquated corner is fashioned in a similar way to my shop, with sections dedicated to cuisines of the world, in alphabetical order, in French. There is an area for children's cookery books and tables throughout displaying new publications. On the opposite side of this room are books organized by subject: bread, soup, etc. And in the corner is a rather large space for the books on wine. I travel upstairs where the focus is professional books with many of the titles in English. Another woman is sitting behind a desk – she does not look up or say boo! I observe many young Japanese women drooling over the pastry books and determine they are attending the cooking school at the Ritz Hotel.

I am happy in this environment and spend a few hours pulling books from the shelves wishing they were all in English. No one tries to converse with me; no Mark Holmes, a welcome fixture at my shop back home, to offer me a cup of tea and a sit down. Momentarily, I am a wee bit homesick. Though really, I am enjoying being in a cookbook shop with no one calling me to the phone or asking me a million questions while I make a mental note of the many books I plan to purchase. But soon I find I do not feel like doing this today any longer. It is time to find a bistro for my *déjeuner*.

I do not want much for lunch as I am dining out tonight. I did not think of asking anyone for a dining recommendation in this neighbourhood, so I cautiously peer into the windows of several cafés before deciding which one deserves my custom. The one I choose has a pleasing menu board outside and appears to have many middle-aged businessmen laughing and happy with their meals. I order a glass of rosé wine, an open-faced sandwich of eggplant and pesto on Poilâne bread, and a simple salad of butter lettuce. It is all delicious and I am content. I spend time writing in my journal before walking back to the flat for a nap.

I am really looking forward to dinner tonight. A friend in Vancouver has reminded me that Kim Campbell is living in Paris and that we should connect. Yes, this is the same Kim Campbell – the only female prime minister of Canada to date. We do know each other, but not well.

Kim and her husband, Hershey Felder, a concert pianist, live in the 6th arrondissement, about a half-hour walk from my flat. Their lives are such that they can live anywhere in the world, and they choose Paris. The apartment is spectacular, built in the 1700s, and other than indoor plumbing and electricity, it is still in its original state. The kitchen has been modernized, but you can imagine how it once looked; it is complete with a door for the "downstairs staff" to enter their place in the home. The sitting room has a grand piano, and Hershey is happy to play Brahms for us. Hershey also loves to cook, but tonight he needs to practise for a concert, so eventually Kim and I head out to a favourite fish restaurant close to their home and we enjoy a lovely dinner. While listening to Kim's adventures and life lessons since her years in federal politics, I am feeling very much like the Wallace Shawn character in the movie *My Dinner with Andre*. And happily, I like this movie very much.

I can imagine Hershey cooking this meal in his lovely kitchen. He would appreciate the menu being very healthy, and very Canadian with French sensibililties.

Steamed Halibut with Crab and Leeks

I like to use a bamboo steamer for this dish. Steamers are available in small sizes and are perfect for the solo cook.

Serves me

Place a bed of arugula in the steamer. On top, place a piece of halibut, about 4 ounces, seasoned lightly with a pinch each of salt and pepper. Place 3 juicy crab legs on top of the halibut.

Mix together 1 heaping tablespoon of thinly sliced leek and 1 teaspoon chopped chives; sprinkle over the crab. Place the steamer over a pan of boiling water and steam for 4 to 5 minutes.

Serve with a salad of arugula and dandelion greens with Mustard Lemon Vinaigrette.

18, February

I am expecting Enrique tonight. He has telephoned almost every day since he left, and yes, an attachment is most certainly forming between us. But he wants to come for eight nights and I am finding this fact incredibly difficult to absorb. Although I am excited to be sure, the reality is I have not spent this much time with anyone, let alone a man, in a very, very long time. And I do have other people I want to see.

I tell myself to stop panicking, stop thinking, STOP analyzing and just let whatever is about to evolve unfold organically.

I manage to find a million things to do outside of the flat today. Flowers; I want to fill the flat with flowers. There is a florist on rue Monge who is very talented; I pick out different varieties and she makes three arrangements for me, all beautiful. I pop into the Eric Kayser *pâtisserie* to purchase *pain au raisin*. I find a charming café to slip into and lean against the bar, Parisian style, to enjoy my *pain* and café crème. While I would never have thought to take a purchase from one shop to eat at another, Enrique taught me on his last visit that doing so is an acceptable custom.

I need some more wine, but not too much as Enrique has particular tastes and I would rather shop for wine with him. In the wine shop on the Île Saint Louis, I am not able to garner much assistance from the merchant who speaks only French, so I take my time to study the labels and choose a wine with the vinaroon label attached to it. This, I know, means it has come from a vineyard where the winemaker is also the farmer who grows and tends the grapes.

I also want to have lots of food on hand. I spend a lot of time in restaurants, and since Enrique is such a good cook and has expressed desire to cook for me, I am happy to oblige. I would love to cook with him, but I'm not sure we are ready for that yet. I have often observed couples who both love to cook competing with each other in the kitchen, and I think it's a good idea to get to know and understand each other's strengths before embracing the dance around the fire together.

We both have work to do: I want to write and he needs to do what he does, mostly over the telephone, so our days are not going to be filled with every other distraction Paris has to offer. We do hope, however, to embark on a few excursions together, so I make a list of ideas to discuss.

It is time for lunch and I want to cook, partly for the joy I will derive from the task, but mostly to separate my thoughts from my nerves.

A little book I love comes to mind: *French Cooking in Ten Minutes,* by Edouard de Pomiane. This book is darling and I want to see if I can make lunch deliciously and efficiently in Pomiane fashion. I have purchased some *charcrute*, which translates to, in this particular case, sauerkraut and two different sausages. I simmer the sausages in a fry pan over medium-low heat for fifteen minutes. Then I tip the water from the pan, leaving the sausages in over low heat, and add the sauerkraut to warm gently for a few minutes, stirring so as not to stick to the pan. As the sausages cook, I wash a large handful of frisée, drying it in a tea towel. I cut five cherry tomatoes into quarters, make a dressing of one tablespoon tarragon mustard, two tablespoons tarragon

mayonnaise and two teaspoons lemon juice. I toss the lettuce and tomatoes with the dressing, arrange the salad on a plate and add the sausages and sauerkraut. Lunch for me, in just over fifteen minutes, is served. Now, you might enjoy a baguette with this meal, but for me, a glass of red wine will suffice.

I have a few more hours before Enrique arrives, so I fill the time with yoga, a long, hot bubble bath, many minutes staring into the closet for the perfect ensemble, and reading some poetry. Finally, for the first time today, I am relaxed, composed and ready for an adventure.

The telephone rings; he is downstairs. Bloody hell.

Oh yes, Paris is most definitely the city to share your love. I am no longer dreaming. *Je suis très content!*

19, FEBRUARY

Breakfast is served in bed and I am very happy to receive it. I am ravenous this morning; we did not really have too much for dinner last night, and we chose to spend the evening chatting while nibbling cheese and fruit, drinking wine.

While we chatted into the wee hours, conversing about many subjects, Enrique casually mentioned he has struggled with cancer. A few years ago, he experienced surgery with bouts of chemotherapy. Now, generally, he feels good, checking in with his doctor on a regular basis. He does not appear to be stressed by this experience in any way, but I do know his love of all food that the good life has to offer is one of his reasons for living — and eating in this manner is not advisable when your body has been tested with serious illness.

But today we are both feeling healthy and happy, ready to explore this beautiful city. We walk to the café and then back to the flat to work for a while. While I tap away on my laptop, I listen to him on the telephone, enthusiastically pitching his ideas and thoughts to whoever is on the other end of the line. Sometimes he is speaking in Spanish, often in French, rarely in English, but I can begin to pick up the nuance in the conversation and can certainly figure out when he is finding it difficult to suffer the fool he is compelled to be talking to.

I decide to make lunch. I love to compose salads and I want to try three simple ideas. The first combination is beetroot and tarragon with an orange honey vinaigrette. (In France you can buy pre-cooked beets everywhere; it is part of the farming culture to cook and package the beets on specially built trucks, in the fields, immediately after they have been harvested. At home I often roast a large quantity of beets at once as they keep well in the refrigerator for a number of days.) The second salad is pear, frisée and walnuts with roquefort dressing. And to complete this ménage à trois, I slice buffalo mozzarella with slightly steamed asparagus and avocado, finishing it with a squeeze of lemon, drizzle of olive oil, lemon salt and freshly ground pepper. I run out to the bakery for baguettes, knowing Enrique believes it unthinkable to eat a meal without bread.

Ménage à Trois (Three Salads)

Here are three pretty, composed salads that need only a few slices of baguette to complete your meal.

Serves me and you

Beets and Tarragon with Honey, Orange and Chive Dressing

I enjoy this salad best after it has rested well together for a while.

To prepare dressing, mix together in a small bowl ½ teaspoon honey, 1½ teaspoons orange juice, ¼ teaspoon orange zest, 1 teaspoon tarragon vinegar and a pinch of salt.

Cook 1 beet in boiling water for 20 minutes. Cut off the tough, woody ends before cutting into 8 wedges. Add to the dressing in the bowl. Tear about 6 lovely tarragon leaves in half and add to the beets. Toss and serve.

Asparagus, Avocado and Buffalo Mozzarella

To prepare dressing, mix together in a medium-size bowl 1 tablespoon olive oil (or better still, avocado oil) and 1 tablespoon lemon juice.

Chop a very little bit of both chives and parsley. Select 7 spears of asparagus and trim to 3 to 4 inches each. Cook spears in boiling water for 1 minute then refresh by rinsing them under cold water. Set aside.

Cut an avocado in 2 and peel one half. Cut the half into 8 chunks. Cut 1 mozzarella ball in half and then into chunks, the same size as the avocado pieces. Add the avocado and mozzarella pieces to the bowl with the dressing. Add the asparagus and mix gently before creatively arranging the salad on a plate. Sprinkle with chives, parsley and lemon salt over top and grind black pepper to taste.

Pear, Frisée and Walnuts with Roquefort Vinaigrette

This recipe calls for 1 pear, but you can use just a portion if the pear is large.

To prepare vinaigrette , mix together in a medium-size bowl 1 tablespoon pear vinegar and 1 tablespoon walnut oil. Stir in 1 heaping tablespoon of crumbled roquefort cheese.

Cut the pear in half and core. Cut the 2 pieces in half again. Peel the skin away, slice into ¼-inch wedges, and then cut the wedges in half. Add to the vinaigrette.

Heat oven to 350° F/180° C. Roast 4 large pieces of walnut for 8 minutes on a baking sheet. Meanwhile, wash a generous handful of frisée and dry in a cloth tea towel. Chop the roasted nuts coarsely and add to the vinaigrette along with the frisée. Mix together gently.

Place salad on plate; grind pepper on top to taste.

After lunch, the glorious weather calls to us. We want to visit la Tour Eiffel; I have never been and Enrique has been just twice, many years ago.

Enrique is the perfect guide for our excursion. We both decide to practise honing our skills in patience as we wait in the lineup for forty-five minutes. Actually, the wait allows us time to truly appreciate this magnificent structure. We finally make our way up the elevator to the second lookout level, and Enrique magically manoeuvres us through the crowd, pointing out monuments of significance from all four sides of the tower. Have I told you I love Paris?

We leave the Eiffel – this memory is a keeper – and head over to rue Cler to shop for food. Enrique wants to cook dinner. I am sure the shopkeepers on rue Cler wish Enrique lived in the neighbourhood. Ecstatically he zips about the various shops and I observe the merchants joyfully fulfilling his wishes to purchase a portion of just about everything. Soon, we are once again laden with tasty packages, and a taxi is hailed to take us home.

20, February

Today I am in for a fine treat. We are literally putting on the Ritz! Enrique has a friend who runs the cooking school at the Ritz Hotel and we are to meet him for lunch to be followed by a tour of the school and kitchens. It is lovely to pull up to the entrance of a fine hotel and be ushered in with such elegance. Pierre meets us in the lobby and we decide to leave the hotel for a bistro Pierre is fond of in the neighbourhood. We enter a stylish café, which is bustling with gregarious customers. We are shown to the table and almost immediately Enrique is incensed. He is appalled with the service, and it gets worse. Potato chips are placed on the table for our amuse(ment). I politely try some of the chips and Enrique admonishes me for eating anything this hideous. The wine list is vapid; the food can only be described as disgusting. I order the salade Niçoise and receive the worst interpretation of this recipe I have given witness to. I feel sorry for Pierre as Enrique asks to speak with the manager to give him a piece of his mind. I am actually quite amused by this Spaniard's sense of loyalty to his memory of a time when it would have been a chore to find a bad place to eat in Paris.

But happily, our good mood is restored when we enter through the service entrance of the Ritz to begin our tour. We observe the students working. As the classes are small, they are blessed with intimate instruction. I find myself wistfully wishing I had come here, to the Ritz in Paris, for my culinary education.

We continue our tour through all the kitchens, meeting chefs and *patissiers*, bakers and butchers. (Did you know that these kitchens were used as a model for the film *Ratatouille*?) We finish our visit in the Bar Vendome with café and petits fours. I express my desire to enjoy a drink in Bar Hemingway, but it does not open until 6·00 p.m. We say goodbye to Pierre, erasing the memory of our lunch; we are delighted with our day. Walking away from the Ritz we decide to stroll around aimlessly for a while, conversing about the list of desires we have concocted, wondering which one to take on next.

We decide that for dinner tonight we should, together, create and make the perfect salade Niçoise. And was it just not the other day I was apprehensive about cooking with a cook?

Our Perfect Salade Niçoise

The leftover tuna in this recipe can be used to make a wonderful sandwich mixed with Lemon Chive Mayonnaise, chopped apple and celery.

Serves me and you

To prepare the vinaigrette, chop 2 canned anchovy fillets and place in a medium-size bowl. Add 2 teaspoons capers, 2 tablespoons lemon juice, ½ teaspoon lemon zest, just under 2 teaspoons Dijon mustard, 2 grinds of pepper and 4 tablespoons extra virgin olive oil. Mix well and set aside, allowing the flavours to meld into each other.

In boiling water cook 2 small eggs for 4 minutes. Set aside to cool; peel and cut into quarters. Take 2 generous handfuls of *haricots verts* (small green beans or French-cut larger green beans) and cook for 1 minute in salted boiling water. Remove from water and refresh for a few seconds in cold water. Steam 10 nugget potatoes for 10 minutes; cool and cut into quarters. Slice 12 cherry tomatoes in half. Open 1 small can of albacore tuna. Select 24 Niçoise olives, and chop 2 tablespoons of curly parsley.

Divide all prepared ingredients for 2 portions, each to be served in a shallow bowl. Place 1 tablespoon of vinaigrette in each bowl, spreading over the bottom. Layer with the tuna, potatoes, beans, olives, tomatoes and eggs, and finish with parsley. Just before serving, gently mix another tablespoon of vinaigrette into the salad, and add a grind of pepper.

Anchovy Butter If you are wondering what to do with the leftover anchovies, I recommend making a prepared butter by blending them in a food processor with 1 pound butter, 2 finely chopped shallots, ½ cup chopped parsley, and ½ cup diced pimento. Roll the mixture into a log, wrap in plastic wrap and freeze until needed.

21, FEBRUARY

Today I am leaving Enrique on his own as I am meeting my friend Michel Roux, a man I adore, at the George V for café. Michel is a chef extraordinaire, owner of the Waterside Inn in Bray, England, and author of many cookery books. Our plan is to share a taxi to the edge of Paris where we will dine with Pat and Bernard Levando in their home for lunch. Bernard owns hotels in Nice, and Michel spends a lot of time in his own home in the south of France, so I imagine they will get along famously. And of course, both Michel and Bernard collect fine wines and boast large cellars. Enrique is appearing to be a little jealous, so I promise to bring Michel back for dinner. Enrique is delighted and he promises to cook something delicious.

I meet Michel and we taxi east to the village of Nogent-sur-Marne, adjacent to the Vincennes, which is what the Bois de Boulongne is to the west of Paris.

We are five for lunch, all lovers of food and wine. Our afternoon begins with a glass of bubbles and nibbles of *saucisson sec*, peanuts and root vegetable chips. Lunch opens with a salad of butter lettuce and a mild, warm goat cheese on a slice of apple. The wine is Château Pavillon Bel-Air, Lalande-de-Pomerol 2001. Next we enjoy sautéed prawns with basmati rice and cold tomato and cucumber with Château Branaire, St. Julien – Medoc 1975. Can you believe my good fortune? We finish the wine with the cheese course, and then in a very merry mood begin our dessert course, which is a delicious chocolate gâteau with a choice of two *glaces* from Berthillon: rum and raisin or chocolate. Of course we all demand both. Then to complete our indulgence, the most beautiful calvados hors d'age is presented, which I decline for myself, although I manage to sneak a few sips from Michel's glass when he is otherwise engaged in conversation.

Michel and I are both a bit sleepy in the taxi ride to my flat on Île de la Cité. We arrive at my flat, not incredibly intent on having anything for dinner, but we agree to pretend we are excited for whatever Enrique has created for us. We decide to walk over to the Île Saint Louis for an aperitif before dinner; the Frenchman and the Spaniard are happy with each other's company, and I am blissful to share this moment with two outstanding men.

We return to the flat for our meal. Neither Michel nor I have asked what we are to expect for dinner, and we share a secret smile when we are presented with a spinach salad and omelette soufflé (Michel's recipe). Enrique intuited that we might return from our lunch over served.

Omelette Soufflé

Enrique said this was Michel Roux's recipe, but we all know Enrique was making it up as he went along because he didn't have Michel's cookbook in hand. However, we all were happy with the result.

I like to serve this dish with a spinach and radish salad composed of a large handful of baby spinach leaves, a few radishes cut into quarters, a dash of salt and a grind of pepper. For the dressing, mix together a squeeze of lemon juice and a few teardrops of olive oil.

Serves me and you

Heat oven to 425° F/220° C.

Separate four large eggs, whipping the whites into submission until hard peaks form. In another bowl, whisk the yolks with 2 teaspoons grainy Dijon mustard, ½ cup grated aged British white cheddar, 2 chopped chives, a dash of salt and a grind of pepper.

In a small stainless steel fry pan, sauté 1 slice of pancetta until crispy. Remove from pan; cool and crumble. Cut 5 cherry tomatoes in half and add to pan to sauté in the pancetta fat for a moment.

Add the pancetta to the egg yolk mixture, then fold the yolks into the whites and place on top of the tomatoes in the fry pan. Cook for 1 minute, then place in the hot oven for about 6 minutes until nicely tanned.

22, February

It is raining on Paris today; feels like home. Actually this flat feels like home, almost like we were born here. And as Enrique, yet again, serves me coffee and breakfast in bed, I realize we have both come to Paris a little lost, longing to give birth to a new stage of contentment. We both have so much to be grateful for in our individual lives, but when one lives too long without identifying one's pain, it is possible to, indeed, become lost. I am beginning to believe that this time we are sharing together is helping to melt the ice that has frozen over the core of both our hearts.

I immediately move from my reflective mode when Enrique announces he wants to take me to the Ritz for Sunday brunch. He understands the buffet to be grand, and would like us both to enjoy the experience.

On the way, we visit the Sunday market on rue du Monge. I love to visit farmers' markets wherever I am, but I really love the markets in Paris, or maybe I love observing the French (and Spanish) mannerisms; they are unique and charming.

Sunday brunch at the Ritz is staged in one of the beautiful rooms usually reserved for special functions. I can imagine the scene in the early morning as each section of the kitchen designs the many tables chosen for their creations, presenting the food beautifully. There is a large rectangular table for fish, a small round one for seafood, another for sushi, *viennoiseries*, salads, and Middle Eastern food, and a hot table dedicated to preparing any egg dish you desire *à la minute*. After we have exhausted those, we venture to the table offering the main course. There are two options: I choose the duck stuffed with foie gras; Enrique has the sea bass in brioche with a crayfish sauce. And we cannot leave without visiting the tables designated for *les pâtisseries*; no, that would be sinful. Another magical moment, sharing each morsel on our individual plates, slowly sipping a bottle of Veuve Clicquot 2002, in such elegant surroundings.

This time we saunter away from the Ritz, wanting a long walk after our indulgence. Although the last thing we need after our decadent lunch is something sweet, when we walk by Ladurée, Enrique insists on buying a dozen *macarons*.

Enrique wants to share with me some of his past memories in Paris, visiting a few of the theatres where he has performed. We do an outside tour this afternoon, deciding to organize some wonderful theatre experience for Tuesday evening.

Enrique is a stage actor. He made a decision early in his career to stay true to this particular medium, wanting no part of film or television. I am enchanted with his ideals while realizing how frustrating these "purist" decisions can be for the creative soul.

He sings to me as we stroll along; I sigh happily. And then I smile, knowing these sensual tones have surely charmed many. I have not had the pleasure of seeing him in a theatre; however, his performance in our Parisian bubble is magnificent.

We have one more excursion planned for this day; we want to visit le Caveau de la Huchette in the Latin Quarter to listen to some live jazz. I think we should go by foot, but Enrique insists it is too far. We walk up to Notre Dame to get a taxi, and the driver is only too happy to make this trip worth his while. It is not until we leave the club that we realize we are about an eight-minute walk from the flat. We double over with laughter and I promise Enrique never to tell a soul about his mishap.

Le Caveau de la Huchette is on two floors; the Clarinette Connection is playing downstairs. We love the music, the scene and the whisky. The history of this building dates back to 1550 and was the particular meeting place for principal figures of the French Revolution: Danton, Marat, Robespierre and others. But since 1946 this historic landmark has been a jazz club and I hope it will stay this way, sharing its magic with music forever.

Today I feel very loved and exceptionally beautiful. Have I told you how happy I am in Paris?

23, FEBRUARY

This evening we are dining out with a friend of Enrique's. The restaurant chosen is Dominique Bouchet, which has a lovely reputation. We dedicate the morning to work, stopping for a light and healthful lunch of broccoli with capers, sliced cold ham, green beans with red pepper vinaigrette and a wedge of brie.

Enrique is happy to make lunch, but I observe him to be edgy and irritated with something that he does not share with me. I am not stressed by this detail; we can't be glowing all the time. But as the day moves along, I agree to accompany him on some errands and I find myself becoming irritated with his behaviour.

Finally we arrive at the restaurant. We are early; his friend has not yet arrived and Enrique orders pink champagne, which most definitely aids in soothing the savage breast. His friend does arrive, and he is a lovely man but he has a terrible cold and he does not speak English. So the two men converse in French and Spanish and I am content to listen to their lovely languages, taking my notebook from my purse to write while waiting for our meal. Enrique decides to order our meals: a lot of food, all very rich. It is mostly delicious; we enjoy cauliflower soup, foie gras, lobster ravioli and beef tenderloin, leaving room for cheese and Grand Marnier soufflé, followed by espresso.

The evening is pleasant enough, and though the food is memorable, this is not my favourite experience in Paris. Enrique is obviously tired and appears to be uncomfortable, so we retire gently, hoping sleep will take us quickly.

I easily fall into slumber, but not for long. Enrique is not well. He is out of his bed much more than in and when the light dawns, he admits to me that he is very sick.

24, February

I am frantic and trying my best not to let it show. Enrique is really ill, and the memories of similar experiences with my mother before she died are overloading my brain. But the maternal instinct I never knew I possessed takes over. There is nothing in the flat that will be helpful; all I can think of is chamomile tea, chicken broth and rice. So I run to the shops as fast as I can to purchase these items. My favourite grocer on the Île Saint Louis is closed, so I head over to the Left Bank. While it is still early for the shops I like, I do find a place open that has what I am looking for.

Back at the flat I brew up the tea and put the rice on to cook. Meanwhile, Enrique has contacted the pharmacy and we make haste to fetch a cure. It is meant to work quickly, but doesn't. Enrique telephones his doctor at home, who telephones the pharmacy with another prescription, so back we go. The day is spent with me trying to feed Enrique soupy rice made with chicken stock. Enrique does manage to sleep a little; I fret a lot. I leave him alone for a while; I need to walk and think. When I return I show Enrique my purchase of a little silver bell. It has two meanings: it can used to summon one's attention, and it will be a reminder of a time when the bells of Notre Dame filled the days of my life.

Enrique is worried about flying home on Thursday, when he has planned to depart, and I tell him if he likes, I will take him home on the train. He starts to rest more comfortably; the drug seems to be working and he falls into slumber.

Later in the day, even though he is still in very rough shape, he insists that he will cook dinner for me tonight. He is feeling bad that we will not make the theatre as planned, and wants to take care of me. So he sends me away to the shops to buy a quail, because I love quail, and because I had expressed a desire for cauliflower gratin and there is a very large cauliflower in the fridge, he is most determined to oblige.

I am not able to change his mind in this matter, so when 6:00 p.m. rolls around, and I make my daily telephone calls home, Enrique rises from his very sick bed to make dinner for me. First he brings me a glass of wine while I am on the telephone. When I am finished I take my wine to the table to observe him cooking for me, helping out when he will let me.

When he presents my dinner to me, I am holding back the tears. He sits at the table with his soupy rice and I am about to enjoy the most memorable meal of my life. A meal made with more love than the quail could hold, but my lord, that quail does its best to contain as much as it can. It is not only a beauty to behold, it is plumper and more succulent than any quail I've ever seen. The cauliflower in the gratin attaches its florets to my fork with such tenderness, covered with a silky sauce that caresses my tongue so lovingly, the taste lingering just long enough until the next bite of quail.

Enrique is so tired and not able to talk or finish his rice. He quietly observes me eating for a long time. My emotional state is fragile and I am eating very slowly. Eventually I convince him to retire while I clean the kitchen.

He is sleeping when I am preparing for bed. I slip under the covers quietly and cry myself to sleep.

Roast Quail

When I'm in Paris, my butcher Jean Paul Gardil (or better yet, his son), working out of his shop at 44 rue Saint Louis en l'île, will take the quail of my choosing, remove the head and burn off the excess feathers and present me with a plump little bundle, ready for my willing oven. I always rinse my birds and let them dry out, in the fridge if I am not planning on cooking immediately, or on the counter if I just can't wait.

Serves me

Heat oven to 375° F/190° C.

Cut ¼ lemon into thin wedges and stuff into the cavity of the quail.

In a small bowl, mix together ¼ teaspoon each of espelette salt, chopped fresh thyme, grape seed oil and a few grinds of black pepper. Rub this mixture all over the quail. (Take your time; it feels good!)

Grease a small roasting pan with 1 teaspoon grape seed oil. Place quail in the pan and roast for about 30 minutes.

Cauliflower Gratin

Serves me and you

Heat oven to 375° F/190° C.

Prepare cauliflower by cutting half of a large head into florets. Steam the cauliflower for 4 minutes, until fork tender. Drain well. Butter a gratin dish and nestle the cauliflower into the dish. Set aside.

Melt 1 tablespoon butter in a small saucepan over medium heat. Whisk in 1 tablespoon flour and cook for 3 to 4 minutes, whisking continuously. Gradually whisk in ¾ cup whole milk and ¾ cup whipping cream. Bring to a gentle boil. Lower the heat and keep whisking for 5 minutes. Season with salt, pepper and ground nutmeg.

Gradually add ¼ cup grated Emmentaler cheese, whisking until the cheese is melted and the sauce is smooth.

Spoon the cheese sauce over the cauliflower. Sprinkle with 2 tablespoons grated Emmentaler and bake in the oven for about 30 minutes. (You can cook the quail and the cauliflower at the same time. They will both come out together with a strong desire to make you happy.)

25, February

Morning is with us, Enrique has rested well and I am not sure I believe him when he says he is feeling much better. He is the strongest man I have ever met – and determined to spend the day pretending he is just fine. Eating is still an issue; naturally he is hesitant. I serve him a cup of chamomile tea, and as the weather is glorious we venture out for a walk along the Seine. But first, we stop at the bakery and Enrique buys a baguette. We go the butcher for a slice of ham, then to the *pâtisserie* for an apple tart. We walk to the wall above the river where Enrique stops to construct a sandwich. He takes one bite, chewing slowly, knowing that if there is going to be a reaction, it will happen quickly. We walk awhile and he is content that his stomach has accepted its offerings, so we head to the café to finish the sandwich and order two espressos, one for me and the other for me. I enjoy the apple tart. We continue our walk along the Seine for a long while. I allow my spirits to fly high and we are both feeling better.

Back at the flat, Enrique rests for a bit before continuing his work in a quieter fashion than usual. I have a meeting to attend; luckily it is very close and will not be long. I want to buy him a present, but I am finding it difficult to think of something appropriate. Walking along rue du Pont Louis Philippe, a street famous for its paper shops, I spot a beautiful box of crayons. I venture in and hand over the thirty-five euros and head back to the flat. Enrique is busy reading through documents. I ask him to stop for a moment so I can give him a present. He grimaces, but I ignore his scowl and tell him I look upon these crayons as a symbol of the rainbow and that I equate the time we have shared to unearthing a pot of gold, and I hope he will use the crayons frequently, choosing different colours for his many moods.

This will be our last night together and I am content to stay in, cook something appropriate, and spend the evening with quiet and thoughtful conversation. But not Enrique. He wants to take me to dinner at Le Dome, because they know him there and he will be allowed to change the menu to suit his pleasure. I argue for a moment, but soon realize it is a futile act, and decide to shut my mouth and head to the bedroom to choose something special to wear for our last supper.

Every day we have spent together I have asked his opinion about my choice of attire, and tonight he responds with the same answer as he has on most occasions, suggesting the Spanish-looking black skirt. I add a low-cut sequined top that he has not seen before and cover it with a shawl until we are seated at the table in the restaurant. He smiles and thanks me for the gesture. I know he is uncomfortable, though his charming character does not alter, and he orders a bottle of wine. I can influence him only in the decision to order lightly as I tell him I am not prepared to eat more than *un petit poisson*. He is quiet, so I fill the void with inconsequential conversation. He listens, nodding yes or no, and then interrupting me to take notice of the two women seated at the next table. They remind us of A. J. Liebling, especially his book *Between Meals: An Appetite for Paris*. These women are most certainly disciples of Liebling's "religion," as they proceed to devour a dozen oysters each, a platter of sea urchins, a large pot of steamed mussels, and Dover sole (not to share – they demand a fish each). For the first time in the long day, I see Enrique's eyes brighten as he delights in observing these two women, aged about sixty, experiencing so much pleasure with their food.

We leave Le Dome before the women embark upon the cheese and dessert course, although I am sure they will choose the mille-feuille, the pastry chef's special creation that is served as a very large portion and is light and airy, but a suitably rich ending to a classically prepared menu.

26, FEBRUARY

The night is not good for Enrique, but dawn arrives and we prepare for his departure. His independent character is in full force and he says he will not require me to assist him home. A taxi arrives and I help him downstairs to the street. Our embrace is a familiar sight to Parisians: lovers parting, silently accepting that the future can only hold the remembrance of a special moment in their lives. Once he is in the car, we wave goodbye to each other.

I have two days left in Paris before I return home. I am in survival mode and decide to keep moving, just like Enrique does.

I had previously organized a cocktail party for twelve guests on this night and decide to stick to the plan. I have the theme and menu already devised, and there is enough wine and champagne in the flat, so all I really need to do is shop for a few ingredients and start cooking. The cure, my cure, for an aching heart – cook and entertain.

Having a kitchen that is not really adequate for entertaining demands an easy menu, one that hopefully my guests will find interesting and tasty. I conceived this menu after walking about Paris with my friend Chris Mooney one day when he stopped to point out a restaurant that he and his wife used to frequent when they were less flush with cash. The name of the restaurant is Dame Tartine, and he described the menu as several different toppings on toast.

This is the menu I prepared for my Dame Tartine affair.

My Dame Tartine Menu

Chopped Chicken Livers with Pancetta
on Toast and Crispy Shallots

•

Roquefort Cheese on Toast with Honey

•

Oven-Roasted Cherry Tomatoes on Toast with Gruyère

•

Duck and Pork Rillettes on Endive

•

Mushroom Soup Served in Small Cups

•

Radishes with French Butter and Citrus Salt

•

Roasted Hazelnuts with Dried Cherries

•

Chocolates and Macarons

I trot over the *pont* to Île Saint Louis to take advantage of my treasured shopping street. First stop is my temple that is the best *boucherie* in Paris, and the butcher's son is a beauty to behold. Most importantly, he knows how to flirt with older women. I purchase the pork and duck rillettes (about half a pound), one pound of chicken livers and one slice of pancetta. Next, off to the vegetable shop where I can purchase a jar of excellent mushroom soup, two jars for twelve people. I need two heads of Belgium endive, one shallot, three dozen cherry tomatoes, three dozen radishes, lemon, parsley and chives. At the creamery, I buy a small wedge of roquefort, the special French butter and a small piece of Gruyère. At the bakery I find a rustic French loaf. I ask the baker to slice the bread very thin for me. Next stop is the *pâtissiere* for twelve assorted small *macarons*.

I need to leave my shopping street to head into the lower Marais district where the shop Izrael is located. The minute you walk into this shop, all your senses are enriched. There is so much here, from spices to condiments, large baskets of lentils and rice, dried and candied fruits, and more. I buy a handful of hazelnuts a few dried cherries and some chocolate-covered orange peel.

Chopped Chicken Livers with Pancetta on Toast and Crispy Shallots

This recipe was inspired from a cookbook called *A Platter of Figs and Other Recipes* written by my friend, chef David Tanis. In his recipe David uses duck livers, and you can also use rabbit livers.

Serves a few

Trim the chicken livers (1 pound) and season with salt and pepper. In a fry pan pour 1 tablespoon of olive oil and add the slice of pancetta, chopped. When nicely browned add livers and turn up the heat. Turn the livers about in the pan for a just a few minutes until they are pink – slice one to check. Then add 1 teaspoon of chopped French thyme and a splash of dry sherry. Put contents onto a cutting board and chop until the mixture is a rough paste. Put into a bowl and add 2 tablespoons of soft butter. Taste for seasoning. Spread the liver mixture on toast rounds and top with Crispy Shallots.

The party is jolly, I can be very good at deception when I put my mind to it. I am grateful that all the guests help me wash up and disappear early, as I am exhausted. I have missed a telephone call from Enrique. He has left me a loving message, advising me he has arrived home, safe.

27, FEBRUARY

I wake up this morning feeling horrid. I am coming down with a cold and have a long list of things I want to accomplish before I leave Paris early tomorrow morning. First though, I must go to my café, for the last time. One of the regular waiters greets me with the usual *bonjour*, but adds a "how are you today" in English. I tell him I am feeling sad because I am leaving Paris tomorrow. We enter into conversation about my work, and when I ask for the bill, he will not let me pay. "Madame, your last breakfast in Paris is on me." I start to cry at this very un-Parisian act.

I head up to Librairie Gourmande to purchase many books to be shipped home. I return to a shop that Enrique and I visited together where he wanted to buy me a black jacket, but I would not let him, even though I really wanted the jacket, so I am back to buy it for myself. I call my friend Chris Mooney and we plan to meet at a café, and I will traipse after him as he visits a number of galleries in the 3rd arrondissement that he needs to write about for his column in the *Art Review*. I meet him with bags of items from my kitchen, which we pack about Paris.

Eventually we make our way to his home, on the fifth floor of a walk-up, and my Paris pantry is laid to rest. Chris decides to concoct a meal with some of my offerings. I enjoy observing his children appreciating every foodstuff presented before them: sardines, squid ink risotto, blinis and smoked salmon. Then they entertain us with acrobatic acts, art projects and recitations of poetry.

I leave to finish packing, planning to meet Chris and his wife, Claire, for one drink at Bar Hemingway in the Ritz Hotel. I decide to arrive early, wanting a few moments on my own to soak up the ambience. There are two levels to this jewel box, about twelve seats on each level. The second level has a bookshelf, well stocked with interesting titles. The walls are wood panelled and well polished. The bar has seven stools. There is one bartender and two servers, all well poised amid this well-worn elegance. The presented menu is unique and states clearly

that it is for sale, for five euros. I order a French 75 — champagne, gin, lemon juice and cointreau — for twenty-eight euros. But before my drink is mixed, I receive a glass of cucumber water, a bowl of roasted almonds, a bowl of olives and a bowl of potato chips. A cloth cocktail napkin is presented when the French 75 is served and *oui*, the drink is superb. I notice a couple, celebrating something special as she opens a beautifully wrapped box containing a very large purse from Miu Miu. They kiss, and I smile.

My friends arrive, and we share my last hours in Paris together in a place I have dreamed of visiting for years.

I arrive home later than expected. I had left a message earlier for Enrique and he has responded at the time I told him would be best to reach me, but I have missed the call, and I sense he is irritated as I listen to his melancholic message.

My Pink Drink

I often torture myself, wanting to introduce new ideas to the world. So instead of giving you a recipe for a French 75, I have devised a drink and asked two seasoned barmen to fine tune it for me. This recipe comprises two of my favourite libations: gin and pink Prosecco. Ah, the desire to feel young, naive and rebellious has returned.

Serves me
In a cocktail shaker pour 1½ ounces gin, ½ ounce Muroise du Val de Loire and ¼ ounce lemon juice. Shake well and do a double strain into a coupe glass. Top with Rosato Prosecco, about 2 ounces, or until your *coupe* is almost full.

28, February

I wake up very early to an alarm, which I do not like to do. I am really unwell this morning but forge ahead. I have a car coming to fetch me for the airport. I am very happy to see Jorge, the man who has been coming weekly to clean the flat for me, arrive to collect the keys and help me with my luggage.

I am numb, really; I feel nothing. I arrive at the airport to a very long line for the security check and manage to stay calm throughout the chaotic manner in which this exercise is conducted. The airplane is going to depart later than expected and I do not care. I am usually nervous before flying, but today I feel no different than if I were to be getting on a bus.

I arrive in Toronto where I plan to spend a few nights with very good friends; for this I am grateful. I am also being met at the airport, and as lovely as this gesture is for me, I feel bad as my hosts will be expecting an enthusiastic meeting, and I am feeling even worse than I was this morning.

My turn comes for the Customs interview and I try to muster the confident posture one wants to express when crossing the border. My luggage is very tightly packed and having to open it for an inspection would be a disaster. I present my passport and Customs form to the officer and he officiously inquires why I spent a month in Paris. I reply, to fall in love. His face softens, and I am quickly sent on my way, with no further interview or inspection requested.

While I am happy to see my friends, intimates I can cry with, I have little energy for sharing my experience. I am in bed early.

The next morning we go out for breakfast and a brisk walk in the sun, bundled up warm as the air in Toronto is insufferably cold. We have our evening meal in; the conversation is subdued. I try to sleep, eventually do, and rise early the next morning to continue my journey home.

2, March

I am home in Vancouver, the city I was born and raised in. The adjustment, leaving Paris where I was incredibly at home, will not be easy. And this wretched cold I have is not helping. But when I open the door to my flat, I feel joy and am pleased to be back in my own jewel box.

I notice that the hearty herbs which are generally comfortable with our winter weather appear sad, but with spring on the way they should bounce back soon and before long I will be able to plant new seeds for my summer kitchen.

My city has grown immensely in recent years; my ever-changing view is very New Yorkish, but when I step onto the deck I can still see mountains to the north, the public library to the northeast, and the community of Mount Pleasant across the Cambie Street Bridge.

My sister has been to visit while I was away and has left my larder full of delicious ingredients. How wonderful for me. So believe it or not, as tired as I am, I want to cook my dinner.

The meal is simple: little pasta ears with pesto (my own from last summer's basil crop) and English (frozen) peas. I toss some salad leaves with lemon and oil, sea salt, and pepper and sit down to a satisfying meal.

As I am enjoying my dinner I realize home, or the genuine feeling of home, is wherever you are happily eating real and well-cooked food.

6, March

There has been no rest for this traveller. I have been back in the shop for four days, and of course there is a lot to catch up on. At the end of these recent days, I have made my way home to rest my weary bones and cook dinner for myself. But tonight I am sick of my own company and feel a great need to confide in a close friend. So I telephone Sally who is happy to hear from me and who can't wait to inquire about the details she felt were missing in my Postcards from Paris blog.

We decide to meet at a French restaurant that is equal walking distance from both of our homes. Le Crocodile is one of my favourite restaurants in Vancouver and I am confident it will take care of two tribulations: missing Paris, and needing to feel grateful to be home, in my city, with the places and people I care about.

Our dinner of braised rabbit is delicious. We linger over our meal with a bottle of wine, and my friend devotes her attention to my tale, offering thoughtful and caring insight. We say goodnight at

the corner of Burrard and Smithe. The evening has been helpful; it felt good to share my story.

~

"~~Life~~ Love is when a person introduces you to yourself for the first time." – Simon Booy

EPILOGUE

One of the first things I do when I return to my shop is hang a map of Paris in my office on the wall above the telephone. When I am asked about my time in Paris, I respond, "It was life altering."

Though initially I don't want to, I need to accept the fact that Enrique is blessed with a supportive family, and my brief encounter with him, nurturing a love one can only appreciate with a cherished soulmate, must now become a treasured memory. It is natural, especially when you are on your own, to allow your heart to close when painful experiences interrupt your life. Giving yourself permission to grieve a loss will support the healing process. But eventually, an opportunity will present itself to you, that only your intuition can determine to be worthy.

Paris was my perfect place to accept the challenge of rediscovering my passion for love and sharing. And now I am adjusting my life to evolve around a reopened heart. I long to return to Paris, though I know it will not resemble this particular month-long occurrence, but for a million other reasons, it will be just as beautiful.

And I may not always choose to live alone, but for as long as I do, I promise to remember, no matter how independent or satisfied I am, I can only achieve great happiness acknowledging that love, in its many forms, is the dominant ingredient for a nourishing and delicious life.

Happy cooking, and here's to elegant sufficiency.

My Paris Address Book

SHOPS

E. Dehillerin
18 Rue Coquillière
75001 Paris, France
01 42 36 53 11
www.e-dehillerin.fr

Eric Kayser
8 Rue Monge
75005 Paris, France
01 44 07 01 42
www.maison-kayser.com

La Grande Épicerie
38 Rue de Sèvres
75007 Paris, France
01 44 39 80 00
www.lagrandeepicerie.fr

Izrael
30 Rue François Miron
75004 Paris, France
01 42 72 66 23

Librairie Gourmande
96 Rue Montmartre
75002 Paris, France
01 43 54 37 27
www.librairiegourmande.fr

Shakespeare and Company
37 Rue de la Bûcherie
75005 Paris, France
01 43 25 40 93
www.shakespeareandcompany.com

Village Voice Bookshop
6 Rue Princesse
75006 Paris, France
01 46 33 25 34
www.villagebookshop.com

CAFÉS AND RESTAURANTS

Le Café des Beaux Arts
7 Quai Malaquais
75006 Paris, France
01 43 54 08 55

Café George V
120 Avenue des Champs-Élysées
75008 Paris, France
01 45 62 33 51

Café Le Lutétia
33 Quai de Bourbon
75004 Paris, France

Café Varenne
36 Rue de Varenne
75007 Paris, France
01 45 48 62 72

My Paris Address Book

Le Caveau de la Huchette
5 Rue de la Huchette
75005 Paris, France
01 43 26 65 05
www.caveaudelahuchette.fr

Les Clos de Gourmets
16 Avenue Rapp
75007 Paris, France
01 45 51 75 61
www.closdesgourmets.com

Le Dome
4 Rue Delambre
75014 Paris, France
01 43 35 34 82

Café les éditeurs
4 Carrefour de l'Odéon
75006 Paris, France
01 43 26 67 76
www.lesediteurs.fr

Gaya par Pierre Gagnaire
44 Rue du Bac
Paris, France
01 45 44 73 73

Ladurée
16 Rue Royale
75008 Paris, France
01 42 60 21 79
www.laduree.fr/public_en/maisons/royale_accueil.htm

Restaurant Dame Tartine
2 Rue Brisemiche
75004 Paris, France
01 42 77 32 22

Restaurant Dominique Bouchet
11 Rue Treilhard
75008 Paris, France
01 45 61 09 46

Ritz Hotel
15 Place Vendôme
75001 Paris, France
01 43 16 30 30
www.ritzparis.com

Saint Amour Café
19 Rue Etienne-Marcel
75001 Paris, France
01 42 33 15 95

Recipes

Apple Armagnac Ice Cream	28
Apple Wedges, Sautéed	28
Anchovy Butter	92
Artichoke Butter	27
Artichoke Dip	43
Asparagus, Avocado and Buffalo Mozzarella Salad	87
Beets and Tarragon with Honey, Orange and Chive Dressing	86
Calamari, Pan-Fried	32
Cauliflower Gratin	105
Chicken Leg, Braised with Niçoise Olives and Tomatoes	20
Chicken Leg, Roasted with Orange Sauce	48
Chicken Livers, Chopped with Pancetta on Toast	112
Chicken Livers with Crispy Shallots	63
Clams, Steamed with Garlic Butter	75
Crab and Turnip Gratin	54
Duck Confit Hash with Sweet Potato	59
Eggs, Scrambled with Sautéed Cherry Tomatoes	34
Endive, Watercress, Frisée and Walnut Salad with Walnut Oil and Sherry Vinaigrette	49
Espelette Salt	7
Fava Bean Succotash	26
Fennel Salad, Roasted with Orange Zest and Parmesan	21
Green Beans, Steamed with Toasted Almonds	69
Halibut, Steamed with Crab and Leeks	80

Leeks Mimosa	12
Lemon Chive Mayonnaise	74
Lemon Salt	7
Mustard Lemon Vinaigrette	55
Omelette Soufflé	95
Orange Salt	7
Pear, Frisée and Walnuts with Roquefort Vinaigrette	88
Pears, Poached with Ginger and Served with Coffee Cream and Ginger Cookies	44
Pink Drink	115
Pink Onion Soup	11
Polenta, Creamy	32
Pork Tenderloin, Roasted with Apple Cider Sauce	44
Quail, Roasted	104
Rabbit Sausages with Fennel, Tarragon and Cherry Tomatoes	40
Rib-Eye Steak, Pan-Roasted	68
Roquefort and Red Pepper Butter	68
Salade Niçoise, Our Perfect	92
Salmon, Smoked and Frisée Salad with Mustard Lemon Vinaigrette	55
Salmon, Wild and Roasted with Artichoke Butter	26
Sausage, Braised with Lentils and Swiss Chard	16
Shallots, Crispy	63
Sole, Fillet Pan-Fried with Sautéed Asparagus	75
Tomato, Onion and Anchovy Salad	15
Watercress Salad with Crab, Tomato, Pancetta and Lemon Chive Mayonnaise	74

Menus

3, February
Pink Onion Soup
Leeks Mimosa

4, February
Tomato, Onion and Anchovy Salad
Braised Sausage and Lentils with Swiss Chard

5, February
Braised Chicken Leg with Niçoise Olives and Tomatoes
Roast Fennel Salad with Orange Zest and Parmesan

6, February
Wild Salmon Roasted with Artichoke Butter and Fava Bean Succotash
Sautéed Apple Wedges
Apple Armagnac Ice Cream

7, February
Pan-Fried Calamari with Creamy Polenta

8, February
Scrambled Eggs with Sautéed Cherry Tomatoes

9, February
Rabbit Sausages with Fennel and Cherry Tomatoes

10, February
Artichoke Dip
Roast Pork Tenderloin with Apple Cider Sauce
Ginger Poached Pears with Coffee Cream
   and Ginger Cookies

11, February
Roast Chicken with Orange Sauce
Endive, Watercress, Frisée and Walnut Salad with Walnut Oil
    and Sherry Vinaigrette

12, February
Crab and Turnip Gratin
Smoked Salmon and Frisée Salad with Mustard Lemon Vinaigrette

13, February
Sweet Potato and Duck Confit Hash

14, February
Chicken Livers with Crispy Shallots

15, February
Pan-Roasted Rib-Eye Steak with Roquefort and Red Pepper Butter
Steamed Green Beans with Toasted Almonds

16, February
Watercress Salad with Crab, Tomato, Pancetta
    and Lemon Chive Mayonnaise
Steamed Clams with Garlic Butter
Pan-Fried Fillet of Sole with Sautéed Asparagus

17, February
Steamed Halibut with Crab and Leeks

19, February
Ménage à Trois (Three Salads)
    Beets and Tarragon with Honey, Orange and Chive Dressing
    Asparagus, Avocado and Buffalo Mozzarella
    Pear, Frisée and Walnuts with Roquefort Vinaigrette

20, February
Our Perfect Salade Niçoise

21, February
 Omelette Soufflé

24, February
 Roast Quail
 Cauliflower Gratin

26, February
 Dame Tartine
  Chopped Chicken Livers with Pancetta on Toast and Crispy Shallots
  Roquefort Cheese on Toast with Honey
  Oven-Roasted Cherry Tomatoes on Toast with Gruyère
  Duck and Pork Rillettes on Endive
  Mushroom Soup Served in Small Cups
  Radishes with French Butter and Citrus Salt
  Roasted Hazelnuts with Dried Cherries
  Chocolates and Macarons

27, February
 My Pink Drink

Acknowledgments

This project began some years ago when my friend David Kent asked me to write a recipe book for people on their own – David was single at the time.

Kirsten Hanson, well-known cookbook editor, encouraged me to write on a more personal level. I took her advice seriously, and as the book took shape in my mind, I realized I would be happy with a wee book about a delicious experience that helped me put my past in its place. And I knew that it would be best to publish this journal for me, by myself.

I convinced a gaggle of supportive friends to read my manuscript. Dalia, Mark, Meeru, Michel, Michele, Patsy, Rozanne, Sally – I thank you all. Not just for your charming comments, but for listening to me ramble on about my life on a regular basis.

And then I put together a crackerjack team of Barb, Lawren, Mark, Bernie, Carol, Michela and Ruth to help me shape this book and get it to the printers.

Finally, I would like to acknowledge the last lines from the poem "Visiting Paris," by Vijay Seshadri: "I didn't stay for the end of the conversation. I was wanted in Paris. Paris, astounded by my splendor and charmed by my excitable manner, waited to open its arms to me."

french apple press
1740 West 2nd Avenue
Vancouver, Canada
V6J 1H6
www.frenchapplepress.com

Copyright © 2010 by Barbara-jo McIntosh

Illustrations copyright © 2010 by Bernie Lyon

All rights reserved. No part of this publication may be reproduced or transmitted
in any form or by any means, electronic or mechanical, including photocopying, recording
or by any information storage and retrieval system, now known or to be invented, without
permission in writing from the publisher.

First french apple press hardcover edition June 2010

For information about ordering and bulk purchases, please contact
Barbara-Jo's Books to Cooks at 604-688-6755
www.bookstocooks.com

The original drawings were created using pencil and the map of Paris
was created using pen and ink.

Editing   Ruth Wilson
Production   Carol Watterson
Recipe testing   Lawren Moneta, Barb Wong, Mark Holmes
Design   Hermani + Sorrentino Design   www.hermanisorrentino.com

Library and Archives Canada Cataloguing in Publication

McIntosh, Barbara-jo

   Cooking for me and sometimes you : a Parisienne romance with recipes / written by
Barbara-jo McIntosh ; illustrated by Bernie Lyon ; edited by Ruth Wilson.

ISBN 978-0-9866031-0-5

   1. McIntosh, Barbara-jo. 2. Cookery, French. 3. Paris (France)--Biography.
I. Title.

TX719.M43 2010   641.5944   C2010-902776-0

This book was printed on FSC-approved paper containing
100% post-consumer recycled fibre, processed chlorine-free.

Printed and bound in Canada by Friesens

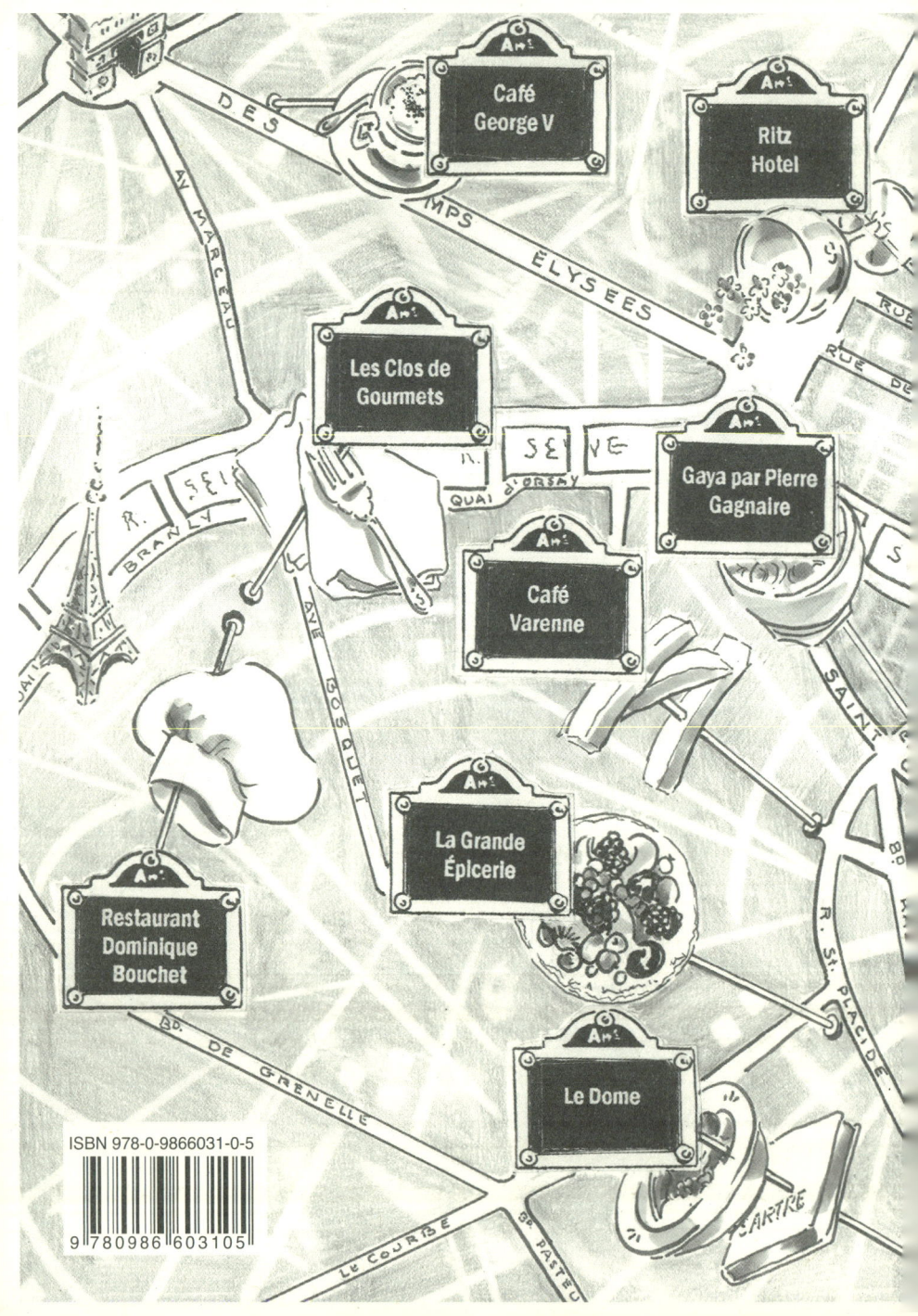